Easy
High Protein Smoothie Recipes Book

Quick & Healthy Blends with Original Ideas & Stunning Photos

Lily Johnson

INTRODUCTION

Welcome to "Easy High-Protein Smoothie Recipes Book: Quick & Healthy Blends with Original Ideas & Stunning Photos" by Lily Johnson, your ultimate guide to transforming your health and energy levels through the power of high-protein smoothies. In this carefully curated collection, Lily Johnson shares her passion for nutrition and wellness, offering you a variety of smoothie recipes that are rich in protein, incredibly delicious, and easy to prepare.

From the bustling professional seeking a quick energy boost to the fitness enthusiast looking for muscle recovery options, this book has something for everyone. Each recipe is accompanied by stunning, full-color photos that will guide you through the process and inspire you to create your own smoothie masterpieces.

Lily's original ideas and tips ensure that you can easily incorporate these smoothies into your daily routine, making healthy living both achievable and enjoyable. Say goodbye to dull and repetitive meals and hello to a world of flavor, health, and energy. Dive into the "Easy High Protein Smoothie Recipes Book" and blend into a healthier you today.

Copyright © 2024 by Lily Johnson

This book or any portion thereof may not be reproduced or used in any manner whatsoever without the author's express written permission except for the use of brief quotations in a book review or scholarly journal. Unauthorized reproduction, sharing, or distribution of this publication or any part thereof may result in legal action against the violator.

The content in this book, including but not limited to text, graphics, images, and other material, is for informational purposes only. This book aims to promote broad consumer understanding and knowledge of various health topics, including but not limited to the benefits of high-protein smoothies. It is not a substitute for professional medical advice, diagnosis, or treatment.

The recipes and information found in this book are the property of Lily Johnson and are protected by United States and international copyright laws. The photographs and illustrations in this publication are included with the permission of the copyright owners and are also protected by copyright laws.

Table of Contents

- Benefits of Smoothie Recipes — Page no - 01
- Why Should You Eat Smoothie Recipes — Page no - 03

Chapter 1: Morning Kickstart Smoothies

- Recipes 01 — Sunrise Strength Shake — Page no - 04
- Recipes 02 — Early Bird Energy Blend — Page no - 06
- Recipes 03 — Breakfast Power Protein — Page no - 08
- Recipes 04 — Morning Glory Muscle Mix — Page no - 10
- Recipes 05 — Wake-Up Whey Wonder — Page no - 12
- Recipes 06 — Dawn Patrol Power-Up — Page no - 14

Chapter 2: Post-Workout Recovery

- Recipes 07 — Muscle Recovery Magic — Page no - 16
- Recipes 08 — Protein Punch Post-Workout — Page no - 18
- Recipes 09 — Fitness Refuel Formula — Page no - 20
- Recipes 10 — After-Exercise Elixir — Page no - 22
- Recipes 11 — Workout Warrior Blend — Page no - 24
- Recipes 12 — Gym Recharge Smoothie — Page no - 26

Chapter 3: Weight Gain Blends

- Recipes 13 — Mass Builder Mix — Page no - 28
- Recipes 14 — Gaining Ground Smoothie — Page no - 30
- Recipes 15 — Protein Packed Power Gainer — Page no - 32
- Recipes 16 — Hearty Bulk-Up Beverage — Page no - 34
- Recipes 17 — Mighty Muscle Mass — Page no - 36
- Recipes 18 — Calorie-Boost Creamy Shake — Page no - 38

Table of Contents

Chapter 4: Lean & Low-Carb

- Recipes (19) Keto Protein Fusion — Page no - 40
- Recipes (20) Lean Machine Mix — Page no - 42
- Recipes (21) Carb-Cut Protein Shake — Page no - 44
- Recipes (22) Slim and Strong Smoothie — Page no - 46
- Recipes (23) Protein-Rich Keto Kick — Page no - 48
- Recipes (24) Lean Green Protein Machine — Page no - 50

Chapter 5: Vegan Protein Varieties

- Recipes (25) Plant-Powered Protein Punch — Page no - 52
- Recipes (26) Vegan Vitality Blend — Page no - 54
- Recipes (27) Green Protein Paradise — Page no - 56
- Recipes (28) Soy Sensation Smoothie — Page no - 58
- Recipes (29) Nutty Vegan Power — Page no - 60
- Recipes (30) Berry Bliss Vegan Shake — Page no - 62

Chapter 6: Antioxidant Infusions

- Recipes (31) Superfood Protein Spectacular — Page no - 64
- Recipes (32) Antioxidant Protein Power — Page no - 66
- Recipes (33) Berry Antioxidant Boost — Page no - 68
- Recipes (34) Fruit Fusion Protein Blend — Page no - 70
- Recipes (35) Tropical Antioxidant Treat — Page no - 72
- Recipes (36) Purple Power Protein — Page no - 74

Chapter 7: Dessert-Inspired Delights

- Recipes (37) Chocolate Peanut Butter Dream — Page no - 76
- Recipes (38) Strawberry Cheesecake Protein Shake — Page no - 78
- Recipes (39) Vanilla Almond Indulgence — Page no - 80

Table of Contents

Recipes (40)	Banana Split Protein Blend	Page no - 82
Recipes (41)	Caramel Apple Protein Twist	Page no - 84
Recipes (42)	Protein Packed Pina Colada	Page no - 86

Chapter 8 : Energy-Boosting Blends

Recipes (43)	Energizer Espresso Protein	Page no - 88
Recipes (44)	Citrus Energy Zing	Page no - 90
Recipes (45)	Tropical Morning Motivator	Page no - 92
Recipes (46)	Mango Tango Energy Shake	Page no - 94
Recipes (47)	Berry Blast Power Smoothie	Page no - 96
Recipes (48)	Green Tea Energy Infusion	Page no - 98

Chapter 9 : Nut Butter Nourishers

Recipes (49)	Peanut Butter Power Smoothie	Page no - 100
Recipes (50)	Almond Joy Protein Shake	Page no - 102
Recipes (51)	Cashew Cream Dream	Page no - 104
Recipes (52)	Nutty Banana Protein Boost	Page no - 106
Recipes (53)	Hazelnut Heaven Smoothie	Page no - 108
Recipes (54)	Pecan Pie Protein Treat	Page no - 110

Chapter 10 : Night-Time Nurturers

Recipes (55)	Sweet Dreams Protein Shake	Page no - 112
Recipes (56)	Moonlight Cherry Almond	Page no - 114
Recipes (57)	Relaxing Vanilla Lavender	Page no - 116
Recipes (58)	Cinnamon Nightcap Protein	Page no - 118
Recipes (59)	Blueberry Evening Elixir	Page no - 120
Recipes (60)	Soothing Coconut Chocolate	Page no - 122

Benefits of Easy High Protein Smoothie Recipes Book

Embark on a delightful journey to health and wellness with Lily Johnson's "Easy High-Protein Smoothie Recipes: Quick & Healthy Blends with Original Ideas & Stunning Photos." This groundbreaking book is designed to transform your approach to nutrition and fitness, offering a delicious path to incorporating more protein into your diet through smoothie making. Whether you want to support muscle recovery, lose weight, or enjoy a nutritious snack or meal replacement, this book is your ultimate companion. Crafted with taste and nutrition in mind, each recipe in this comprehensive collection combines a variety of fresh and wholesome ingredients to create smoothies that are as nourishing as they are delicious. From the velvety richness of chocolate and peanut butter to the tropical zest of mango and coconut, Lily Johnson provides an array of flavors that will satisfy any palate. What sets this book apart is its focus on high-protein content and the meticulous attention to detail in every recipe. Lily Johnson has gone to great lengths to ensure that each smoothie is balanced, easy to prepare, and accessible to everyone, regardless of dietary restrictions or preferences.

Benefits of Easy High Protein Smoothie Recipes Book

Inside this vibrant book, you'll discover: Over 60 innovative high-protein smoothie recipes, each accompanied by stunning, full-color photography that will inspire and entice you. Detailed nutritional information for each recipe allows you to easily track your daily protein intake and vital nutrients.

Expert tips on selecting the best ingredients, customizing recipes to your taste, and achieving the perfect smoothie consistency every time. Insightful advice on integrating these high-protein smoothies into your daily routine, whether as a meal replacement, a post-workout recovery drink, or a healthy snack.

Easy High-Protein Smoothie Recipes" is more than a cookbook; it's a guide to enhancing your health and enjoying the process. Lily Johnson's passion for nutrition and delicious food shines through on every page, making this book a joy to read and an essential tool in your culinary arsenal. Join countless others in discovering how simple and enjoyable it can be to make high-protein smoothies a part of your daily life and take the first step towards a healthier, happier you.

Why Should You Eat Easy High-Protein Smoothie Recipes

Delight in nutritious and convenient refreshments with "Why Should You Eat Easy High-Protein Smoothie Recipes" by Lily Johnson. This essential recipe book introduces a collection of delectable smoothie concoctions designed to fuel your day with protein-packed goodness. Whether aiming to jumpstart your mornings or refuel after a workout, these smoothies offer a delicious and convenient solution.

Lily Johnson expertly crafts each recipe to ensure maximum flavor and nutritional value, making it easy to maintain a balanced diet without sacrificing taste. Packed with essential vitamins, minerals, and high-quality proteins, these smoothies are perfect for busy individuals seeking a quick and healthy meal.

With clear instructions and readily available ingredients, whipping up these smoothies is a breeze, catering to beginners and seasoned smoothie enthusiasts alike. Embrace a healthier lifestyle with these easy-to-make, protein-rich smoothie recipes. Whether you prefer Kindle or paperback, "Why Should You Eat Easy High Protein Smoothie Recipes" is your go-to guide for nutritious and delicious blends. Grab your copy today and revolutionize your approach to healthy eating.

Chapter 1 : Morning Kickstart Smoothies

Recipe 1 : Sunrise Strength Shake Smoothies

Energize your mornings with the Sunrise Strength Shake, a high-protein smoothie designed to kickstart your day. This nutrient-packed beverage is an ideal breakfast choice for those leading an active lifestyle or anyone needing a quick, healthy, and satisfying morning meal. Combining delicious flavors and powerful proteins, it's the perfect way to fuel your body and start your day with a burst of energy.

Servings: 1 (One)

Prepping Time: 5 Minutes

Cook Time: 0 Minutes

Difficulty: Easy

INGREDIANT

- 1 scoop protein powder (vanilla or chocolate)
- 1 cup unsweetened almond milk
- 1/2 ripe banana
- 1/4 cup Greek yogurt
- 1 tbsp almond butter
- 1 tsp honey (optional)
- 1/2 tsp ground cinnamon
- Ice cubes (optional)

NUTRITIONAL FACTS: (PER SERVING)

Calories: 320	Protein: 26g
Carbohydrates: 25g	Fat: 12g
Fiber: 4g	Sugar: 10g

STEP BY PREPARATION

- Place protein powder, almond milk, banana, Greek yogurt, almond butter, honey (if using), and cinnamon in a blender.
- Add ice cubes for a thicker shake, if desired.
- Blend on high until smooth and creamy.
- Pour into a glass and enjoy immediately.

The "Sunrise Strength Shake" is more than a drink; it's a powerful tool for wellness and vitality. Whether post-workout or just beginning your day, this shake provides the perfect balance of protein, healthy fats, and carbs to energize and satisfy you. Its rich, creamy texture and natural sweetness make it a deliciously effective way to achieve your health and fitness goals.

Chapter 1 : Morning Kickstart Smoothies

Recipe 2 : Early Bird Energy Blend Smoothies

Start your day with the refreshing "Early Bird Energy Blend Smoothie," a high-protein concoction designed to wake you up and fuel your morning. This smoothie is perfect for those seeking a quick, nutritious breakfast or a pre-workout energy boost. It combines a blend of wholesome ingredients to kickstart your metabolism and keep you energized, making it an ideal choice for health-conscious individuals on the go.

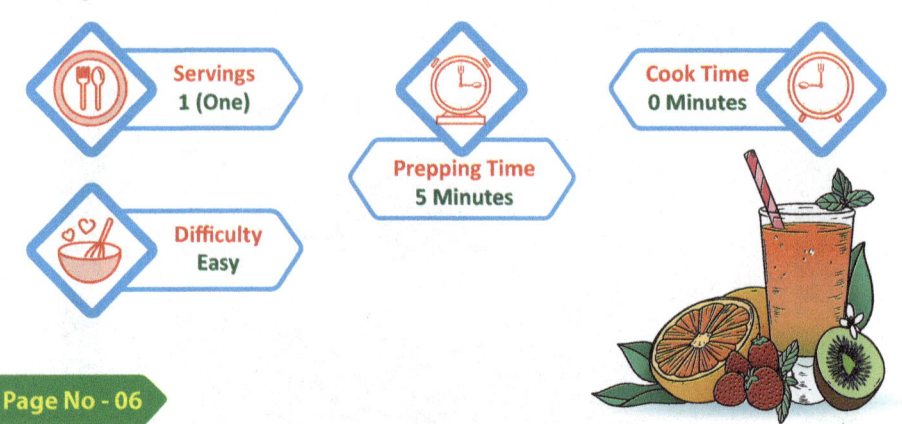

Servings: 1 (One)

Prepping Time: 5 Minutes

Cook Time: 0 Minutes

Difficulty: Easy

INGREDIANT

- 1 scoop vanilla protein powder
- 1 cup cold brewed coffee
- 1/2 banana, preferably frozen
- 1/4 cup rolled oats
- 1 tbsp almond butter
- 1/2 tsp cinnamon
- Ice cubes (optional)

NUTRITIONAL FACTS: (PER SERVING)

Calories: 360	Protein: 30g
Carbohydrates: 40g	Fat: 10g
Fiber: 5g	Sugar: 10g

STEP BY PREPARATION

- Add the protein powder, cold brewed coffee, banana, rolled oats, almond butter, and cinnamon to a blender.
- If a colder consistency is desired, add a few ice cubes.
- Blend on high until the mixture becomes smooth and creamy.
- Serve the smoothie in a tall glass or on-the-go container.

The "Early Bird Energy Blend Smoothie" is your ideal morning partner, offering a delicious blend of flavors and essential nutrients. Whether preparing for an intense workout or needing an energy lift to start your day, this smoothie provides the perfect combination of protein, healthy fats, and complex carbohydrates. Enjoy its creamy texture and satisfying taste as you embark on your daily activities.

Chapter 1 : Morning Kickstart Smoothies

Recipe 3 : Breakfast Power Protein Smoothies

Jumpstart your morning with the "Breakfast Power Protein Smoothie," a robust and nutrient-dense drink designed to fuel your day. Ideal for those on a fitness journey or anyone seeking a hearty and healthful start, this high-protein smoothie blends delicious flavors with essential nutrients. It's a fantastic choice for a quick and satisfying breakfast, providing the energy and protein you need to tackle your day head-on.

Servings
1 (One)

Prepping Time
5 Minutes

Cook Time
0 Minutes

Difficulty
Easy

INGREDIANT

- ☑ 1 scoop chocolate or vanilla
- ☑ protein powder
- ☑ 1 cup almond milk
- ☑ 1/2 ripe banana
- ☑ 1/4 cup Greek yogurt
- ☑ 1 tbsp peanut butter
- ☑ 1 tbsp chia seeds
- ☑ A handful of spinach leaves
- ☑ Ice cubes (optional)

NUTRITIONAL FACTS: (PER SERVING)

Calories: 350	Protein: 15g
Carbohydrates: 20g	Fat: 25g
Fiber: 6g	Sugar: 10g

STEP BY PREPARATION

- ▶ Combine protein powder, almond milk, banana, Greek yogurt, peanut butter, chia seeds, and spinach in a blender.
- ▶ Add ice cubes if you prefer a colder smoothie.
- ▶ Blend on high until smooth and creamy.
- ▶ Pour into a glass and enjoy immediately.

The "Breakfast Power Protein Smoothie" is an excellent way to ensure you're well-nourished and ready for whatever challenges the day may bring. It's the perfect blend for a post-workout recovery or a quick breakfast fix, providing a balanced mix of protein, healthy fats, and carbs. Enjoy its rich, smooth taste and natural sweetness as you set a positive and energetic tone for your day.

Chapter 1 : Morning Kickstart Smoothies

Recipe 4 : Morning Glory Muscle Mix Smoothies

Embark on your day with the "Morning Glory Muscle Mix Smoothie," a high-protein blend perfect for kickstarting your morning with vigor. Ideal for fitness enthusiasts or anyone seeking a nutrient-rich breakfast, this smoothie combines delicious, healthful ingredients to provide a balanced and energizing start. It's an excellent choice for a quick breakfast or a nourishing post-workout drink, loaded with protein and flavor.

- **Servings:** 1 (One)
- **Prepping Time:** 5 Minutes
- **Cook Time:** 0 Minutes
- **Difficulty:** Easy

INGREDIANT

- ✓ 1 scoop vanilla protein powder
- ✓ 1 cup coconut water
- ✓ 1/2 cup frozen mixed berries
- ✓ 1/4 cup rolled oats
- ✓ 1 tbsp almond butter
- ✓ 1/2 banana
- ✓ A handful of spinach
- ✓ Ice cubes (optional)

NUTRITIONAL FACTS: (PER SERVING)

Calories: 350	Protein: 25g
Carbohydrates: 40g	Fat: 10g
Fiber: 6g	Sugar: 15g

STEP BY PREPARATION

▶ Place protein powder, coconut water, mixed berries, rolled oats, almond butter, banana, and spinach in a blender.

▶ Add ice cubes for additional chill and thickness, if desired.

▶ Blend until smooth and creamy. Serve in your favorite glass for an immediate energy boost.

The "Morning Glory Muscle Mix Smoothie" is more than just a breakfast drink; it's a nutrient powerhouse, perfect for those leading an active lifestyle. Whether heading out for a workout or starting a busy day, this smoothie is packed with everything you need to stay energized and satisfied. Enjoy its smooth, creamy texture and the sweet, natural taste of fruits and nuts as you begin your day.

Chapter 1 : Morning Kickstart Smoothies

Recipe 5 : Wake-Up Whey Wonder Smoothies

Energize your mornings with the "Wake-Up Whey Wonder Smoothie," a high-protein blend designed to jumpstart your day. Perfect for those seeking a quick, nutritious, and satisfying breakfast option, this smoothie is packed with the goodness of whey protein, fruits, and other wholesome ingredients. It's ideal for fitness enthusiasts or anyone needing a morning energy boost, providing a delicious and healthful start to the day.

- **Servings**: 1 (One)
- **Prepping Time**: 5 Minutes
- **Cook Time**: 0 Minutes
- **Difficulty**: Easy

INGREDIANT

- ✅ 1 scoop whey protein powder (vanilla or chocolate)
- ✅ 1 cup unsweetened almond milk
- ✅ 1/2 ripe banana
- ✅ 1/4 cup Greek yogurt
- ✅ 1 tbsp natural peanut butter
- ✅ 1 tsp ground flaxseed
- ✅ A pinch of cinnamon
- ✅ Ice cubes (optional)

NUTRITIONAL FACTS: (PER SERVING)

Calories: 360	Protein: 30g
Carbohydrates: 30g	Fat: 14g
Fiber: 4g	Sugar: 12g

STEP BY PREPARATION

- ▶ Combine whey protein powder, almond milk, banana, Greek yogurt, peanut butter, flaxseed, and cinnamon in a blender.
- ▶ Add ice cubes for a thicker consistency, if preferred.
- ▶ Blend on high until the mixture is smooth.
- ▶ Pour the smoothie into a glass and enjoy immediately.

The "Wake-Up Whey Wonder Smoothie" is a fantastic way to ensure you're well-equipped to face the day. Whether you're gearing up for a workout or need a fulfilling meal to start your day, this smoothie strikes the perfect balance of taste and nutrition. Its rich, creamy texture and hint of sweetness make it a healthful choice and a delightful morning treat.

Chapter 1 : Morning Kickstart Smoothies

Recipe 6 : Dawn Patrol Power-Up Smoothies

Start your day on a high note with the "Dawn Patrol Power-Up Smoothie," a perfect blend for those early mornings when you need an extra boost. This high-protein smoothie is ideal for anyone looking to kickstart their day with a nutritious and delicious beverage. It's packed with ingredients that provide energy and protein, making it a great choice for morning workouts or a busy day ahead.

Servings: 1 (One)
Prepping Time: 5 Minutes
Cook Time: 0 Minutes
Difficulty: Easy

INGREDIANT

- 1 scoop of protein powder (choice of flavor)
- 1 cup of cold brewed coffee
- 1/2 frozen banana
- 1/4 cup rolled oats
- 1 tbsp almond butter
- 1 tsp cocoa powder
- 1/2 tsp vanilla extract
- Ice cubes (optional)

NUTRITIONAL FACTS: (PER SERVING)

Calories: 375	Protein: 28g
Carbohydrates: 40g	Fat: 12g
Fiber: 5g	Sugar: 10g

STEP BY PREPARATION

- In a blender, combine the protein powder, cold brewed coffee, frozen banana, rolled oats, almond butter, cocoa powder, and vanilla extract.
- Add ice cubes for a chilled smoothie, if desired.
- Blend on high until smooth and creamy.
- Serve in a glass and savor immediately.

The "Dawn Patrol Power-Up Smoothie" is not just a drink; it's a morning ritual that prepares you for whatever lies ahead. Whether you're an early riser heading to the gym or need a substantial breakfast to fuel your morning, this smoothie is the perfect combination of taste and health, setting you up for a successful day.

Chapter 2 : Post-Workout Recovery

Recipe 7 : Muscle Recovery Magic Smoothies

Rejuvenate and refuel after your workout with the " Muscle Recovery Magic Smoothie," a high-protein drink designed to aid muscle recovery and replenish your energy. Perfect for fitness enthusiasts and athletes, this smoothie is a blend of nourishing ingredients that support post-exercise recovery. It's ideal for those seeking a quick, delicious, and effective way to recover after intense physical activity.

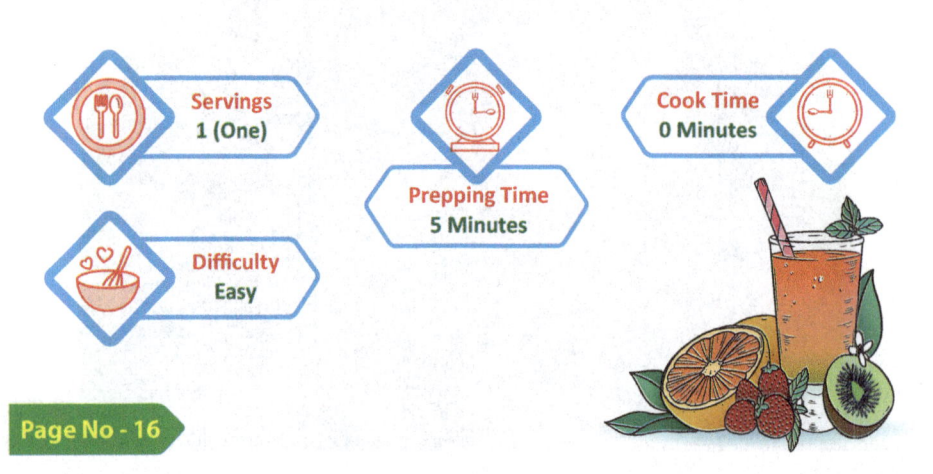

- **Servings**: 1 (One)
- **Prepping Time**: 5 Minutes
- **Cook Time**: 0 Minutes
- **Difficulty**: Easy

INGREDIANT

- 1 scoop whey protein powder (chocolate or vanilla)
- 1 cup almond milk (unsweetened)
- 1/2 banana, frozen
- 1/4 cup Greek yogurt
- 1 tbsp almond butter
- 1 tsp honey (optional)
- A pinch of cinnamon
- Ice cubes (optional)

NUTRITIONAL FACTS: (PER SERVING)

Calories: 350	Protein: 28g
Carbohydrates: 30g	Fat: 12g
Fiber: 3g	Sugar: 15g

STEP BY PREPARATION

- Combine the whey protein powder, almond milk, frozen banana, Greek yogurt, almond butter, honey (if using), and a pinch of cinnamon.
- Add ice cubes for a thicker consistency, if desired.

  Blend until smooth and creamy.
- Serve immediately for the best recovery benefits.

The " Muscle Recovery Magic Smoothie" is your go-to post-workout companion, offering a perfect balance of protein, healthy fats, and carbohydrates. Not only does it aid in muscle recovery, but it also satisfies your taste buds with its rich and creamy texture. It's a convenient and tasty way to ensure you give your body the nutrients it needs after a workout.

Chapter 2 : Post-Workout Recovery

Recipe 8 : Protein Punch Post-Workout Smoothies

Refuel effectively after your workout with the "Protein Punch Post-Workout Smoothie," a high-protein, nutrient-rich drink designed to accelerate recovery. Ideal for athletes and fitness enthusiasts, this smoothie offers a perfect blend of protein, carbs, and essential nutrients to replenish your body and support muscle repair. It's an excellent choice for anyone looking for a quick, delicious, and adequate post-exercise nourishment.

Servings
1 (One)

Prepping Time
5 Minutes

Cook Time
0 Minutes

Difficulty
Easy

INGREDIANT

- 1 scoop protein powder (flavor of choice)
- 1 cup coconut water
- 1/2 ripe banana
- 1/4 cup frozen mixed berries
- 1 tbsp ground flaxseed
- 1 tsp honey or agave syrup
- Ice cubes (as needed)

NUTRITIONAL FACTS: (PER SERVING)

Calories: 320	Protein: 25g
Carbohydrates: 40g	Fat: 5g
Fiber: 4g	Sugar: 20g

STEP BY PREPARATION

- Add protein powder, coconut water, banana, mixed berries, ground flaxseed, and honey/agave syrup to a blender.
- Include ice cubes for a more relaxed texture, if preferred.
- Blend on high until smooth and creamy.
- Pour the smoothie into a glass and enjoy post-workout.

The "Protein Punch Post-Workout Smoothie" is your ideal workout partner, helping you recover faster and more effectively. It's a treat for your muscles and a delight for your taste buds. Enjoy its refreshing taste and creamy texture as you give your body the post-workout care it deserves.

Chapter 2 : Post-Workout Recovery

Recipe 9 : Fitness Refuel Formula Smoothies

Recharge your body after a rigorous workout with the "Fitness Refuel Formula Smoothie," a high-protein drink for optimal post-exercise recovery. Tailored for fitness enthusiasts, this smoothie balances proteins, carbs, and essential nutrients, aiding muscle recovery and replenishing energy. It's an excellent option for anyone seeking a quick, nutritious, and delicious way to refuel after physical activity.

- **Servings**: 1 (One)
- **Prepping Time**: 5 Minutes
- **Cook Time**: 0 Minutes
- **Difficulty**: Easy

INGREDIANT

- ✅ 1 scoop of your preferred protein powder
- ✅ 1 cup skim milk or almond milk
- ✅ 1/2 frozen banana
- ✅ 1/4 cup Greek yogurt
- ✅ 1 tbsp almond butter
- ✅ 1 tsp chia seeds
- ✅ A pinch of ground ginger
- ✅ Ice cubes (optional)

NUTRITIONAL FACTS: (PER SERVING)

Calories: 380	Protein: 30g
Carbohydrates: 35g	Fat: 10g
Fiber: 4g	Sugar: 15g

STEP BY PREPARATION

- ▶ In a blender, combine protein powder, milk, frozen banana,
- ▶ Greek yogurt, almond butter, chia seeds, and ginger.
- ▶ Add ice cubes if a chilled smoothie is preferred.
- ▶ Blend until smooth and creamy.
- ▶ Pour into a glass and enjoy it as a post-workout treat.

The "Fitness Refuel Formula Smoothie" is not just a beverage; it's a recovery tool, perfect for replenishing your body after intense physical exertion. Its combination of flavors and nutrients makes it a delightful way to end your workout, ensuring you're nourishing your body while enjoying a delicious, creamy smoothie.

Chapter 2 : Post-Workout Recovery

Recipe 10 : After-Exercise Elixir Smoothies

Revitalize your body post-exercise with the "After-Exercise Elixir Smoothie," a high-protein concoction designed to aid recovery and replenish energy. This smoothie is perfect for athletes and fitness enthusiasts, offering a delicious blend of ingredients that promote muscle repair and rehydration. It's ideal for those seeking a quick, nourishing, and tasty way to recuperate after a strenuous workout session.

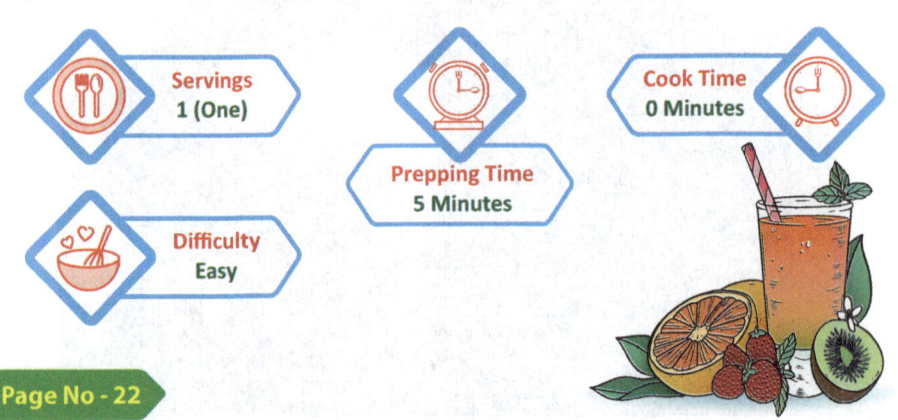

- **Servings**: 1 (One)
- **Prepping Time**: 5 Minutes
- **Cook Time**: 0 Minutes
- **Difficulty**: Easy

INGREDIANT

- ✅ 1 scoop protein powder (flavor of choice)
- ✅ 1 cup coconut water
- ✅ 1/2 ripe avocado
- ✅ 1/4 cup fresh pineapple chunks
- ✅ 1 tbsp flaxseed oil
- ✅ 1 tsp honey (optional)
- ✅ A few mint leaves
- ✅ Ice cubes (optional)

NUTRITIONAL FACTS: (PER SERVING)

Calories: 400	Protein: 25g
Carbohydrates: 30g	Fat: 20g
Fiber: 5g	Sugar: 15g

STEP BY PREPARATION

- ▶ Combine protein powder, coconut water, avocado, pineapple, flaxseed oil, honey (if using), and mint leaves in a blender.
- ▶ Add ice cubes if you prefer a colder smoothie.
- ▶ Blend until smooth and consistent.
- ▶ Serve immediately for maximum post-workout benefits.

The "After-Exercise Elixir Smoothie" is your perfect post-workout companion, balancing taste with nutritional value. It's a treat for your taste buds and a boon for your body, helping you recover faster and more effectively. Enjoy this smoothie as a delightful and healthful conclusion to your workout routine.

Chapter 2 : Post-Workout Recovery

Recipe 11 : Workout Warrior Blend Smoothies

Unleash the power of recovery with the "Workout Warrior Blend Smoothie," designed for high protein post-workout nourishment. This smoothie is a perfect blend for athletes and fitness enthusiasts who need an effective way to replenish energy and aid muscle recovery after intense training. Its combination of protein, carbs, and essential nutrients makes it an ideal choice for those dedicated to their fitness journey.

- **Servings:** 1 (One)
- **Prepping Time:** 5 Minutes
- **Cook Time:** 0 Minutes
- **Difficulty:** Easy

INGREDIANT

- 1 scoop of chocolate protein powder
- 1 cup almond milk
- 1/2 frozen banana
- 1/4 cup cooked and cooled sweet potato
- 1 tbsp natural peanut butter
- 1 tsp cocoa powder
- A pinch of sea salt
- Ice cubes (optional)

NUTRITIONAL FACTS: (PER SERVING)

Calories: 350	Protein: 30g
Carbohydrates: 35g	Fat: 10g
Fiber: 5g	Sugar: 15g

STEP BY PREPARATION

- Place protein powder, almond milk, banana, sweet potato, peanut butter, cocoa powder, and sea salt in a blender.
- Add ice cubes for a thicker texture, if desired.
- Blend until smooth and creamy.
- Pour the smoothie into a glass and savor post-workout.

The "Workout Warrior Blend Smoothie" is a great way to ensure you get the proper post-workout recovery nutrients. Its creamy texture and rich chocolate flavor make it a delightful treat, while its balanced nutritional profile supports muscle repair and energy replenishment. It's the perfect smoothie to help you stay on track with your fitness and health goals.

Chapter 2 : Post-Workout Recovery

Recipe 12 : Gym Recharge Smoothie

Reenergize after your workout with the "Gym Recharge Smoothie," a perfect high-protein blend to aid your post-workout recovery. This smoothie is an excellent choice for gym-goers and fitness enthusiasts looking for an efficient refuel. Packed with proteins and essential nutrients, it not only aids in muscle recovery but also replenishes your energy, making it an indispensable part of your fitness regime.

Servings
1 (One)

Prepping Time
5 Minutes

Cook Time
0 Minutes

Difficulty
Easy

INGREDIANT

- ✓ 1 scoop vanilla protein powder
- ✓ 1 cup unsweetened almond milk
- ✓ 1/2 ripe banana
- ✓ 1/4 cup Greek yogurt
- ✓ 1 tbsp almond butter
- ✓ 1 tsp honey (optional)
- ✓ 1/2 tsp cinnamon
- ✓ Ice cubes (optional)

NUTRITIONAL FACTS: (PER SERVING)

Calories: 350	Protein: 30g
Carbohydrates: 32g	Fat: 12g
Fiber: 4g	Sugar: 18g

STEP BY PREPARATION

- ▶ Combine protein powder, almond milk, banana, Greek yogurt, almond butter, honey (if using), and cinnamon in a blender.
- ▶ Add ice cubes if you prefer an excellent smoothie.
- ▶ Blend until smooth.
- ▶ Pour into a glass and enjoy it as a refreshing post-workout drink.

The "Gym Recharge Smoothie" is your ultimate post-exercise replenishment. Its balanced mix of protein, healthy fats, and carbohydrates ensures a rapid recovery and a boost in energy levels. This delicious and creamy smoothie is a treat for your muscles and a delight for your taste buds, perfectly rounding off your workout routine.

Chapter 3 : Weight Gain Blends

Recipe 13 : Mass Builder Mix Smoothie

Fuel your muscle-building journey with the "Mass Builder Mix Smoothie," a high-protein, nutrient-packed drink for those focused on gaining weight and muscle mass. This smoothie is a powerhouse of calories and protein, making it ideal for athletes, bodybuilders, or anyone looking to bulk up. It's nutritious and delicious, offering a satisfying way to consume the extra calories and protein needed for mass gain.

- **Servings:** 1 (One)
- **Prepping Time:** 5 Minutes
- **Cook Time:** 0 Minutes
- **Difficulty:** Easy

INGREDIANT

- ✓ 2 scoops of high-calorie protein powder
- ✓ 1 cup whole milk
- ✓ 1/2 cup rolled oats
- ✓ 1 ripe banana
- ✓ 2 tbsp peanut butter
- ✓ 1 tbsp honey
- ✓ 1 tbsp chia seeds
- ✓ 1/4 cup Greek yogurt

NUTRITIONAL FACTS: (PER SERVING)

Calories: 950	Protein: 60g
Carbohydrates: 80g	Fat: 40g
Fiber: 10g	Sugar: 35g

STEP BY PREPARATION

- ▶ Add protein powder, whole milk, rolled oats, banana, peanut butter, honey, chia seeds, and Greek yogurt to a blender.
- ▶ Blend on high speed until smooth and creamy.
- ▶ Adjust the thickness by adding more milk if necessary.
- ▶ Pour into a large glass and enjoy.

The "Mass Builder Mix Smoothie" is your perfect ally in the quest for muscle gain. Its blend of high-calorie ingredients provides the necessary fuel to support your intense workouts and muscle growth. Enjoy this delicious, creamy smoothie as a convenient way to meet your dietary goals and power through your muscle-building journey.

Chapter 3 : Weight Gain Blends

Recipe 14 : Gaining Ground Smoothie

The "Mass Builder Mix Smoothie" is your perfect ally in the quest for muscle gain. Its blend of high-calorie ingredients provides the necessary fuel to support your intense workouts and muscle growth. Enjoy this delicious, creamy smoothie as a convenient way to meet your dietary goals and power through your muscle-building journey.

- **Servings:** 1 (One)
- **Prepping Time:** 5 Minutes
- **Cook Time:** 0 Minutes
- **Difficulty:** Easy

INGREDIANT

- ✓ 2 scoops vanilla protein powder
- ✓ 1 cup whole milk
- ✓ 1 ripe banana
- ✓ 1/4 cup rolled oats
- ✓ 2 tbsp almond butter
- ✓ 1 tbsp honey
- ✓ 1/4 cup Greek yogurt
- ✓ A pinch of cinnamon

NUTRITIONAL FACTS: (PER SERVING)

Calories: 800	Protein: 55g
Carbohydrates: 70g	Fat: 35g
Fiber: 8g	Sugar: 30g

STEP BY PREPARATION

- ▶ In a blender, combine protein powder, whole milk, banana, rolled oats, almond butter, honey, Greek yogurt, and cinnamon.
- ▶ Blend until smooth and creamy. If needed, adjust the consistency by adding more milk.
- ▶ Pour into a large glass and consume immediately.

The "Gaining Ground Smoothie" is an excellent way to ensure you get the right balance of nutrients to support your weight gain and muscle-building journey. It's a perfect option for a post-workout recovery drink or a nutrient-rich snack, helping you meet your calorie and protein needs deliciously and satisfyingly.

Chapter 3 : Weight Gain Blends

Recipe 15 : Protein Packed Power Gainer Smoothie

Elevate your muscle-building regimen with the "Protein Packed Power Gainer Smoothie," a high-protein concoction formulated explicitly for weight gain and muscle enhancement. This smoothie is an excellent choice for athletes, bodybuilders, or anyone aiming to increase their protein intake and caloric density. It combines various ingredients to create a delicious, nourishing, and effective way to support your fitness goals.

Servings
1 (One)

Prepping Time
5 Minutes

Cook Time
0 Minutes

Difficulty
Easy

INGREDIANT

- ✓ 2 scoops of whey protein powder
- ✓ 1 cup of whole milk
- ✓ 1/2 cup of Greek yogurt
- ✓ 1 ripe banana
- ✓ 2 tbsp of peanut butter
- ✓ 1 tbsp of honey
- ✓ 1 tbsp of ground flaxseed
- ✓ A sprinkle of cinnamon

NUTRITIONAL FACTS: (PER SERVING)

Calories: 90	Protein: 65g
Carbohydrates: 75g	Fat: 35g
Fiber: 7g	Sugar: 40g

STEP BY PREPARATION

- ▶ Add whey protein powder, whole milk, Greek yogurt, banana, peanut butter, honey, ground flaxseed, and cinnamon to a blender.
- ▶ Blend everything until smooth and thoroughly mixed.
- ▶ Add more milk if you need to adjust the thickness.
- ▶ Serve in a large glass for immediate enjoyment.

The "Protein Packed Power Gainer Smoothie" is your perfect ally in your weight gain journey. It's loaded with high-quality proteins and tastes great, making your path to achieving a muscular physique both delicious and effective. Whether a post-workout recovery drink or a nutritious snack, this smoothie is a great way to fuel your fitness pursuits.

Chapter 3 : Weight Gain Blends

Recipe 16 : Hearty Bulk-Up Beverage Smoothie

Energize your muscle growth and weight gain journey with the "Hearty Bulk-Up Beverage Smoothie." This high-protein drink is masterfully crafted for those looking to add mass and muscle efficiently. Packed with nourishing ingredients, it's ideal for bodybuilders, athletes, or anyone needing a calorie-dense, protein-rich dietary addition. Enjoy this delicious smoothie as a tasty and effective way to meet your fitness and weight gain goals.

Servings: 1 (One)
Prepping Time: 5 Minutes
Cook Time: 0 Minutes
Difficulty: Easy

INGREDIANT

- 2 scoops protein powder (vanilla or chocolate)
- 1 cup whole milk
- 1 ripe banana
- 2 tbsp natural peanut butter
- 1/4 cup rolled oats
- 1 tbsp honey or maple syrup
- 1 tbsp chia seeds
- A dash of vanilla extract

NUTRITIONAL FACTS: (PER SERVING)

Calories: 850	Protein: 60g
Carbohydrates: 80g	Fat: 30g
Fiber: 8g	Sugar: 35g

STEP BY PREPARATION

- Place protein powder, whole milk, banana, peanut butter, rolled oats, honey/maple syrup, chia seeds, and vanilla extract in a blender.
- Blend until the mixture becomes smooth and creamy.
- Adjust consistency with more milk if needed.
- Serve in a large glass and enjoy immediately.

The "Hearty Bulk-Up Beverage Smoothie" is an excellent addition to your muscle-building diet. It offers a delightful mix of taste and nutrition, making your goal of gaining mass a delicious journey. Whether as a post-workout recovery drink or a meal replacement, this smoothie provides the perfect combination of high-quality protein and essential nutrients.

Chapter 3 : Weight Gain Blends

Recipe 17 : Mighty Muscle Mass Smoothie

Embark on your muscle-building journey with the "Mighty Muscle Mass Smoothie," a high-protein powerhouse designed for those striving to gain weight and build muscle. This smoothie is the perfect blend for athletes, bodybuilders, or anyone looking to enhance their dietary intake with a calorie-rich, nutritious drink. It's effective for mass gain and irresistibly delicious, making it a favorite for your fitness

Servings
1 (One)

Prepping Time
5 Minutes

Cook Time
0 Minutes

Difficulty
Easy

INGREDIANT

- ✅ 2 scoops of chocolate protein powder
- ✅ 1 cup of whole milk
- ✅ 1 ripe banana
- ✅ 1/4 cup of oats
- ✅ 2 tbsp of almond butter
- ✅ 1 tbsp of honey
- ✅ 1 tbsp of cocoa powder
- ✅ A pinch of cinnamon

NUTRITIONAL FACTS: (PER SERVING)

Calories: 800	Protein: 55g
Carbohydrates: 70g	Fat: 30g
Fiber: 9g	Sugar: 30g

STEP BY PREPARATION

- ▶ In a blender, combine protein powder, milk, banana, oats, almond butter, honey, cocoa powder, and cinnamon.
- ▶ Blend on high until the texture is smooth and creamy.
- ▶ Adjust the thickness by adding more milk if needed.
- ▶ Serve the smoothie in a large glass for immediate consumption

The "Mighty Muscle Mass Smoothie" is a nutritional powerhouse, perfect for fuelling your body post-workout or as a substantial snack. Its delicious taste and creamy texture make it a delightful way to meet your higher calorie and protein needs. This smoothie is a drink and a crucial tool in your arsenal for building strength and muscle mass.

Chapter 3 : Weight Gain Blends

Recipe 18 : Calorie-Boost Creamy Shake Smoothie

Boost your calorie intake with the "Calorie-Boost Creamy Shake," a high-protein smoothie designed to gain weight and muscle. Ideal for athletes and bodybuilders, this nutrient-rich shake combines the goodness of protein with calorie-dense ingredients, offering a delicious way to supplement your diet. It's an excellent choice for anyone who needs a convenient, tasty, and effective solution for weight gain.

- Servings: 1 (One)
- Prepping Time: 5 Minutes
- Cook Time: 0 Minutes
- Difficulty: Easy

INGREDIANT

- 2 scoops of vanilla protein powder
- 1 cup of full-fat milk
- 1 ripe banana
- 1/4 cup of heavy cream
- 2 tbsp of peanut butter
- 1 tbsp of honey
- 1 tsp of vanilla extract
- Ice cubes (optional)

NUTRITIONAL FACTS: (PER SERVING)

Calories: 950	Protein: 60g
Carbohydrates: 80g	Fat: 45g
Fiber: 5g	Sugar: 50g

STEP BY PREPARATION

- Blend protein powder, full-fat milk, banana, heavy cream, peanut butter, honey, and vanilla extract in a blender.
- Add ice cubes for a chilled effect, if desired.
- Blend until smooth and creamy.
- Pour the shake into a large glass and enjoy immediately.

The "Calorie-Boost Creamy Shake" is not just a smoothie; it's a strategic approach to weight gain and muscle building. It's perfect for those who struggle to consume enough calories through regular meals, providing a delicious and efficient way to increase your intake. Enjoy this creamy, satisfying shake as part of your daily routine to achieve your fitness and health goals.

Chapter 4 : Lean & Low-Carb

Recipe 19 : Keto Protein Fusion Smoothie

Embrace a healthy, low-carb lifestyle with the "Keto Protein Fusion Smoothie," designed for those following a ketogenic diet or seeking a high-protein, low-carbohydrate meal option. This smoothie supports weight loss goals while ensuring adequate protein intake. It's a fantastic choice for a nutritious breakfast, a post-workout refuel, or a satisfying snack, blending great taste with keto-friendly ingredients.

- Servings: 1 (One)
- Prepping Time: 5 Minutes
- Cook Time: 0 Minutes
- Difficulty: Easy

INGREDIANT

- ✅ 1 scoop of low-carb vanilla protein powder
- ✅ 1 cup of unsweetened almond milk
- ✅ 1/2 avocado
- ✅ 1 tbsp of almond butter
- ✅ 1 tsp of chia seeds
- ✅ A pinch of cinnamon
- ✅ Ice cubes (optional)

NUTRITIONAL FACTS: (PER SERVING)

Calories: 300	Protein: 25g
Carbohydrates: 10g	Fat: 20g
Fiber: 5g	Sugar: 1g

STEP BY PREPARATION

- ▶ Combine protein powder, almond milk, avocado, almond butter, chia seeds, and cinnamon in a blender.
- ▶ Add ice cubes for a more relaxed texture, if preferred.
- ▶ Blend until smooth and creamy.
- ▶ Pour into a glass and enjoy it as a nourishing keto-friendly drink.

The "Keto Protein Fusion Smoothie" is a beautiful addition to your keto diet, offering a balance of high-quality protein and healthy fats while keeping the carbs low. Its creamy texture and subtly sweet taste make it a delightful and convenient way to stick to your dietary goals, ensuring you stay energized and satisfied.

Chapter 4 : Lean & Low-Carb

Recipe 20 : Lean Machine Mix Smoothie

Step up your health game with the "Lean Machine Mix Smoothie," a high-protein, lean, and low-carb delight. This smoothie is an excellent choice for those on a weight loss journey, following a low-carb diet, or simply seeking a nutritious and filling meal replacement. It blends a perfect mix of ingredients to support your fitness goals while tantalizing your taste buds with its delicious flavor.

Servings
1 (One)

Prepping Time
5 Minutes

Cook Time
0 Minutes

Difficulty
Easy

INGREDIANT

- 1 scoop of low-carb protein powder (flavor of choice)
- 1 cup unsweetened almond milk
- 1/2 cup frozen mixed berries
- 1/4 cup spinach
- 1 tbsp ground flaxseed
- 1/2 tsp vanilla extract
- Ice cubes (optional)

NUTRITIONAL FACTS: (PER SERVING)

Calories: 250	Protein: 20g
Carbohydrates: 15g	Fat: 10g
Fiber: 5g	Sugar: 5g

STEP BY PREPARATION

- Add protein powder, almond milk, mixed berries, spinach, ground flaxseed, and vanilla extract to a blender.
- Include ice cubes for a more refreshing taste, if desired.
- Blend on high until smooth and creamy.
- Serve in a glass and relish this nourishing smoothie.

The "Lean Machine Mix Smoothie" is your ideal partner in achieving a healthier, leaner physique. It's a nutritious option for your dietary needs and a delightful way to enjoy a guilt-free treat. Whether post-workout or need a quick meal, this smoothie is a perfect blend of health and flavor.

Chapter 4 : Lean & Low-Carb

Recipe 21 : Carb-Cut Protein Shake Smoothie

The "Carb-Cut Protein Shake" is a dream come true for those on a low-carb diet, offering a delicious blend of high protein and minimal carbohydrates. This smoothie is perfect for anyone looking to maintain muscle mass while cutting carbs, making it an ideal choice for weight loss regimes, keto diets, or post-workout nutrition. It's a simple, tasty, and effective way to stay on track with your health goals.

Servings: 1 (One)

Prepping Time: 5 Minutes

Cook Time: 0 Minutes

Difficulty: Easy

INGREDIANT

- 1 scoop of low-carb protein powder (vanilla or chocolate)
- 1 cup unsweetened almond milk
- 1/4 cup Greek yogurt
- 1 tbsp almond butter
- 1 tsp cocoa powder (if using vanilla protein powder)
- A pinch of stevia or preferred sweetener
- Ice cubes (optional)

NUTRITIONAL FACTS: (PER SERVING)

Calories: 280	Protein: 25g
Carbohydrates: 10g	Fat: 15g
Fiber: 4g	Sugar: 3g

STEP BY PREPARATION

- Blend protein powder, almond milk, Greek yogurt, almond butter, cocoa powder, and sweetener in a blender.
- Add ice cubes for a chilled shake, if desired.
- Blend until smooth and creamy.
- Pour into a glass and enjoy immediately.

The Carb-Cut Protein Shake is more than just a smoothie; it's a nutritional strategy for those dedicated to a fit and healthy lifestyle. It's the perfect way to enjoy a delicious and satisfying treat without compromising your dietary goals, whether you want to lose weight, build muscle, or maintain a balanced diet.

Chapter 4 : Lean & Low-Carb

Recipe 22 : Slim and Strong Smoothie

Embrace a healthier lifestyle with the Slim and Strong Smoothie, a perfect blend for those seeking a high-protein, low-carb option. Ideal for fitness enthusiasts or anyone on a weight management journey, this smoothie offers a delicious way to nourish your body while supporting your fitness goals. It's a beautiful choice for a quick, nutritious breakfast or a post-workout replenishment, balancing great taste with health benefits.

- **Servings:** 1 (One)
- **Prepping Time:** 5 Minutes
- **Cook Time:** 0 Minutes
- **Difficulty:** Easy

INGREDIANT

- ✅ 1 scoop of vanilla or chocolate protein powder
- ✅ 1 cup unsweetened almond milk
- ✅ 1/2 avocado
- ✅ 1 tbsp chia seeds
- ✅ 1 tsp unsweetened cocoa powder (if using vanilla protein)
- ✅ A pinch of cinnamon
- ✅ Ice cubes (optional)

NUTRITIONAL FACTS: (PER SERVING)

Calories: 300	Protein: 25g
Carbohydrates: 12g	Fat: 18g
Fiber: 7g	Sugar: 1g

STEP BY PREPARATION

- ▶ Combine protein powder, almond milk, avocado, chia seeds, cocoa powder (if using), and cinnamon in a blender.
- ▶ Add ice cubes for a thicker consistency, if preferred.
- ▶ Blend until smooth and creamy.
- ▶ Pour into a glass and enjoy immediately.

The "Slim and Strong Smoothie" is not just a beverage; it's a tool for maintaining a healthy and balanced diet. Its creamy texture and rich flavor make it a delightful way to stay on track with your dietary goals. Whether you're aiming for weight loss or muscle tone, this smoothie is a delicious and effective way to achieve your objectives.

Chapter 4 : Lean & Low-Carb

Recipe 23 : Protein-Rich Keto Kick Smoothie

Discover the perfect fusion of taste and nutrition with the "Protein-Rich Keto Kick Smoothie," specially designed for those on a ketogenic diet or anyone seeking a high-protein, low-carb meal option. This smoothie is excellent for maintaining energy levels while sticking to your keto goals. It's ideal for a quick breakfast, a pre-workout boost, or a post-exercise replenishment, offering a delicious and convenient way to stay aligned with your health and fitness aspirations.

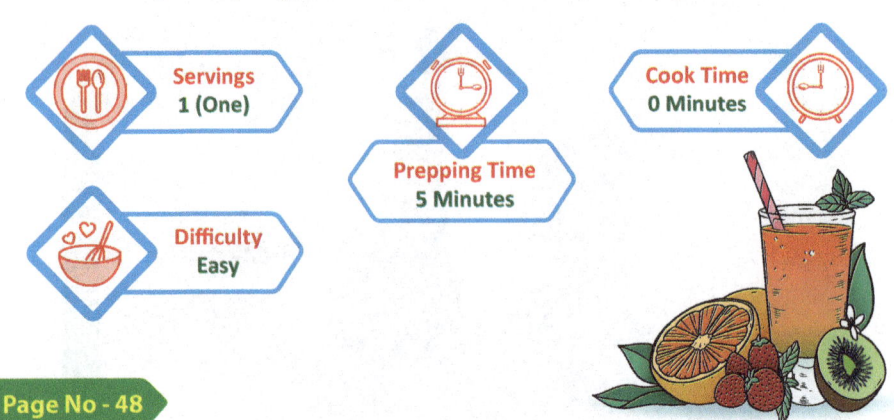

- **Servings:** 1 (One)
- **Prepping Time:** 5 Minutes
- **Cook Time:** 0 Minutes
- **Difficulty:** Easy

INGREDIANT

- ✅ 1 scoop of low-carb protein powder (vanilla or chocolate)
- ✅ 1 cup unsweetened almond milk
- ✅ 1/2 ripe avocado
- ✅ 1 tbsp coconut oil
- ✅ 1 tsp unsweetened cocoa powder
- ✅ (if using vanilla protein)
- ✅ A pinch of cinnamon
- ✅ Stevia or preferred sweetener to taste
- ✅ Ice cubes (optional)

NUTRITIONAL FACTS: (PER SERVING)

Calories: 320	Protein: 25g
Carbohydrates: 8g	Fat: 22g
Fiber: 5g	Sugar: 1g

STEP BY PREPARATION

▶ Place protein powder, almond milk, avocado, coconut oil, cocoa powder (if using), cinnamon, and sweetener in a blender.

▶ Add ice cubes if a more excellent smoothie is preferred.

▶ Blend until it reaches a smooth and creamy consistency.

▶ Pour into a glass and enjoy your keto-friendly smoothie.

The "Protein-Rich Keto Kick Smoothie" is more than just a meal; it's a delicious way to support your ketogenic lifestyle. Its combination of high-quality protein and healthy fats makes it a satisfying option to keep you fueled and focused throughout the day, ensuring you stay on track with your keto journey.

Chapter 4 : Lean & Low-Carb

Recipe 24 : Lean Green Protein Machine Smoothie

Kickstart your wellness journey with the "Lean Green Protein Machine Smoothie," a perfect concoction for those seeking a high-protein, low-carb dietary option. Ideal for health enthusiasts and fitness lovers, this smoothie combines nutrient-rich greens with protein powder, offering a rejuvenating boost to your day. Whether you're looking for a post-workout recovery drink or a nourishing meal replacement, this smoothie is a healthy and delicious choice.

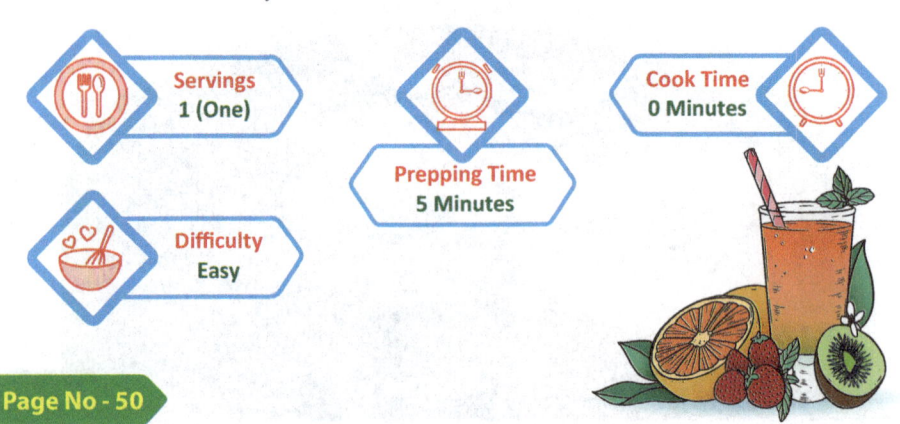

Servings 1 (One)

Prepping Time 5 Minutes

Cook Time 0 Minutes

Difficulty Easy

INGREDIANT

- ✅ 1 scoop of plant-based protein powder
- ✅ 1 cup unsweetened almond milk
- ✅ 1/2 cup fresh spinach
- ✅ 1/4 avocado
- ✅ 1/2 cucumber, sliced
- ✅ 1 tbsp chia seeds
- ✅ Juice of 1/2 lemon
- ✅ Ice cubes (optional)

NUTRITIONAL FACTS: (PER SERVING)

Calories: 280	Protein: 20g
Carbohydrates: 15g	Fat: 15g
Fiber: 8g	Sugar: 3g

STEP BY PREPARATION

- ▶ Combine protein powder, almond milk, spinach, avocado, cucumber, chia seeds, and lemon juice in a blender.
- ▶ Add ice cubes for a chilled smoothie, if desired.
- ▶ Blend until smooth and creamy.
- ▶ Serve in a tall glass and enjoy immediately.

The "Lean Green Protein Machine Smoothie" is more than just a drink; it's a step towards a healthier, more balanced lifestyle. Packed with essential nutrients and vitamins, it's an excellent way to ensure you get your daily dose of greens while enjoying a delicious and fulfilling meal. Perfect for any time of the day, it's a great way to fuel your body and mind.

Chapter 5 : Vegan Protein Varieties

Recipe 25 : Plant-Powered Protein Punch Smoothie

Dive into the plant-based goodness with the "Plant-Powered Protein Punch Smoothie," a vegan delight designed to boost your protein intake using purely plant-based sources. This smoothie is perfect for vegans, vegetarians, or anyone interested in a healthy, animal-free protein option. It combines delicious and nutritious ingredients, providing an ideal blend for a post-workout refreshment or a wholesome start to your day.

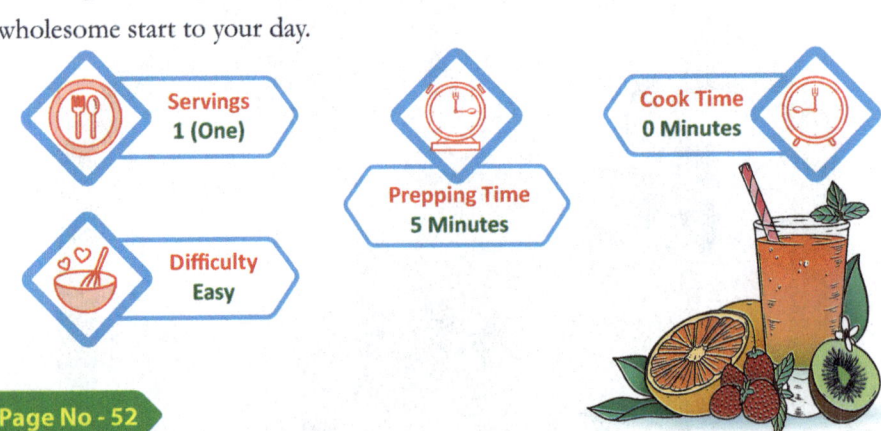

Servings: 1 (One)
Prepping Time: 5 Minutes
Cook Time: 0 Minutes
Difficulty: Easy

INGREDIANT

- 1 scoop of vegan protein powder (flavor of choice)
- 1 cup unsweetened almond milk
- 1/2 ripe banana
- 1/4 cup frozen mixed berries
- 1 tbsp ground flaxseed
- 1 tbsp almond butter
- A handful of spinach leaves
- Ice cubes (optional)

NUTRITIONAL FACTS: (PER SERVING)

Calories: 320	Protein: 20g
Carbohydrates: 30g	Fat: 12g
Fiber: 6g	Sugar: 12g

STEP BY PREPARATION

- Blend protein powder, almond milk, banana, mixed berries, flaxseed, almond butter, and spinach in a blender.
- Add ice cubes for a cooler, thicker smoothie, if desired.
- Blend until smooth and creamy.
- Pour into a glass and enjoy the vegan protein boost.

The "Plant-Powered Protein Punch Smoothie" is not just a beverage but a testament to the power of plant-based nutrition. Whether you're a dedicated vegan or simply exploring healthier alternatives, this smoothie is a delicious way to incorporate more plant-based protein into your diet. It's a delightful fusion of taste and health, making your journey to wellness both enjoyable and nutritious.

Chapter 5 : Vegan Protein Varieties

Recipe 26 : Vegan Vitality Blend Smoothie

Welcome to the world of vibrant health with the "Vegan Vitality Blend Smoothie," a perfect mix for those seeking a high-protein, plant-based nutritional boost. This smoothie is an excellent choice for vegans, vegetarians, and health-conscious individuals looking for a delicious way to incorporate more plant-based protein into their diets. Packed with natural, wholesome ingredients, it's ideal for a nourishing start to the day or a replenishing post-workout treat.

- **Servings:** 1 (One)
- **Prepping Time:** 5 Minutes
- **Cook Time:** 0 Minutes
- **Difficulty:** Easy

INGREDIANT

- ✓ 1 scoop vegan protein powder (flavor of choice)
- ✓ 1 cup unsweetened soy milk
- ✓ 1/2 ripe banana
- ✓ 1/4 cup blueberries (fresh or frozen)
- ✓ 1 tbsp chia seeds
- ✓ 1 tbsp peanut butter
- ✓ A handful of kale or spinach
- ✓ Ice cubes (optional)

NUTRITIONAL FACTS: (PER SERVING)

Calories: 350	Protein: 25g
Carbohydrates: 35g	Fat: 12g
Fiber: 7g	Sugar: 15g

STEP BY PREPARATION

- ▶ Place protein powder, soy milk, banana, blueberries, chia seeds, peanut butter, and kale/spinach in a blender.
- ▶ Add ice cubes for a chilled smoothie, if preferred.
- ▶ Blend until smooth and creamy.
- ▶ Serve in a glass and savor the plant-powered goodness.

The "Vegan Vitality Blend Smoothie" is more than just a drink; it celebrates health and wellness. It's a convenient and tasty way to ensure you're getting a balance of essential nutrients while following a plant-based diet. Enjoy this smoothie as a delicious testament to the power and taste of vegan nutrition.

Chapter 5 : Vegan Protein Varieties

Recipe 27 : Green Protein Paradise Smoothie

Embark on a nutritious journey with the "Green Protein Paradise Smoothie," a delightful blend perfect for those embracing a vegan lifestyle or seeking a plant-based protein boost. This smoothie is an excellent choice for anyone looking to add a healthy, protein-rich twist to their diet. It combines the freshness of greens with the power of plant protein, making it ideal for a rejuvenating breakfast or a post-workout recharge.

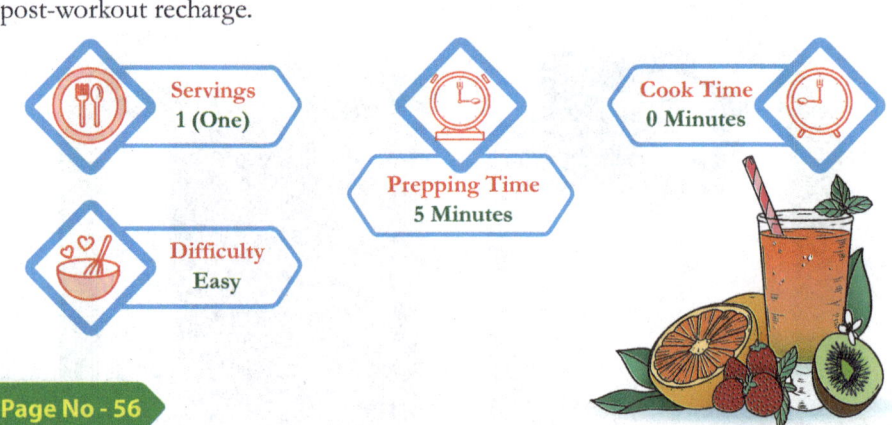

- Servings: 1 (One)
- Prepping Time: 5 Minutes
- Cook Time: 0 Minutes
- Difficulty: Easy

INGREDIANT

- 1 scoop of plant-based protein powder
- 1 cup unsweetened almond milk
- 1/2 cup fresh spinach
- 1/2 ripe avocado
- 1/4 cup cucumber, chopped
- 1 tbsp ground flaxseed
- 1 tsp lemon juice
- Ice cubes (optional)

NUTRITIONAL FACTS: (PER SERVING)

Calories: 300	Protein: 20g
Carbohydrates: 20g	Fat: 15g
Fiber: 3g	Sugar: 3g

STEP BY PREPARATION

- Mix protein powder, almond milk, spinach, avocado, cucumber, flaxseed, and lemon juice in a blender.
- Add ice cubes for a more excellent smoothie, if desired.
- Blend until smooth and creamy.
- Pour into a glass and enjoy this green protein treat.

The "Green Protein Paradise Smoothie" is your ticket to a healthier, more vibrant lifestyle. It's not just a nutritious choice; it's a delicious way to enjoy the benefits of vegan protein. Whether you're a committed vegan or just exploring healthier options, this smoothie perfectly blends taste and wellness, keeping you nourished and satisfied.

Chapter 5 : Vegan Protein Varieties

Recipe 28 : Soy Sensation Smoothie

Dive into the delightful world of vegan nutrition with the "Soy Sensation Smoothie," a high-protein blend perfect for those on a plant-based diet. This smoothie is a fantastic choice for vegans or anyone interested in a dairy-free protein boost. It combines the nutritional power of soy with other wholesome ingredients, offering a delicious and healthy addition to your daily routine, whether as a meal replacement or a post-workout refreshment.

- Servings: 1 (One)
- Prepping Time: 5 Minutes
- Cook Time: 0 Minutes
- Difficulty: Easy

INGREDIANT

- ✅ 1 scoop of soy protein powder
- ✅ 1 cup unsweetened soy milk
- ✅ 1/2 ripe banana
- ✅ 1/4 cup strawberries (fresh or frozen)
- ✅ 1 tbsp almond butter
- ✅ 1 tsp flaxseed meal
- ✅ A dash of vanilla extract
- ✅ Ice cubes (optional)

NUTRITIONAL FACTS: (PER SERVING)

Calories: 350	Protein: 25g
Carbohydrates: 30g	Fat: 12g
Fiber: 5g	Sugar: 12g

STEP BY PREPARATION

- ▶ Add soy protein powder, milk, banana, strawberries, almond butter, flaxseed meal, and vanilla extract to a blender.
- ▶ Include ice cubes for a chilled smoothie, if desired.
- ▶ Blend until smooth and creamy.
- ▶ Serve in a glass and savor the rich, plant-based protein goodness.

The "Soy Sensation Smoothie" is more than just a beverage; it's a testament to the delicious possibilities of vegan nutrition. Whether fully committed to a plant-based diet or exploring healthier alternatives, this smoothie is a beautiful way to incorporate high-quality vegan protein into your diet, ensuring you stay energized and satisfied throughout the day.

Chapter 5 : Vegan Protein Varieties

Recipe 29 : Nutty Vegan Power Smoothie

Embark on a healthful journey with the "Nutty Vegan Power Smoothie," a high-protein, plant-based delight designed to energize and nourish. This smoothie is an excellent pick for vegans, fitness enthusiasts, or anyone looking for a dairy-free protein source. It's packed with natural, nutty flavors and essential nutrients, making it perfect for a quick breakfast, an energizing snack, or a post-workout recharge.

Servings: 1 (One)

Prepping Time: 5 Minutes

Cook Time: 0 Minutes

Difficulty: Easy

INGREDIANT

- 1 scoop vegan protein powder (pea or soy-based)
- 1 cup unsweetened almond milk
- 1/2 ripe banana
- 2 tbsp almond butter
- 1 tbsp chia seeds
- 1 tsp hemp seeds
- A pinch of cinnamon
- Ice cubes (optional)

NUTRITIONAL FACTS: (PER SERVING)

Calories: 400	Protein: 25g
Carbohydrates: 30g	Fat: 20g
Fiber: 6g	Sugar: 10g

STEP BY PREPARATION

- Combine protein powder, almond milk, banana, almond butter, chia seeds, hemp seeds, and cinnamon in a blender.
- Add ice cubes for a colder and thicker consistency, if preferred.
- Blend until smooth.
- Pour into a glass and enjoy the nutty, protein-rich smoothie.

The "Nutty Vegan Power Smoothie" is more than just a beverage; it boosts plant-based power. Whether embracing a vegan lifestyle or simply seeking healthier options, this smoothie is a delicious way to fuel your body with essential nutrients. Its rich, creamy texture and satisfying taste make it a delightful addition to your daily routine.

Chapter 5 : Vegan Protein Varieties

Recipe 30 : Berry Bliss Vegan Shake Smoothie

Indulge in the delightful "Berry Bliss Vegan Shake," a smoothie that combines the richness of berries with the power of vegan protein. This high-protein, plant-based treat is perfect for anyone looking to enjoy a delicious, dairy-free protein boost. Whether you're a vegan, a fitness enthusiast, or just exploring healthier options, this smoothie offers a refreshing blend of taste and nutrition, ideal for any time of the day.

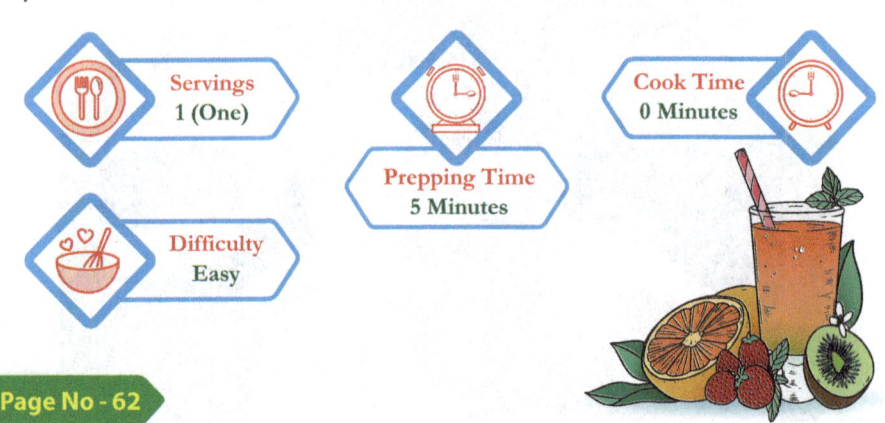

- **Servings** 1 (One)
- **Prepping Time** 5 Minutes
- **Cook Time** 0 Minutes
- **Difficulty** Easy

INGREDIANT

- 1 scoop vegan protein powder (berry flavored or plain)
- 1 cup unsweetened almond milk
- 1/2 cup mixed berries (fresh or frozen)
- 1/4 avocado
- 1 tbsp ground flaxseed
- A few mint leaves
- Ice cubes (optional)

NUTRITIONAL FACTS: (PER SERVING)

Calories: 350	Protein: 25g
Carbohydrates: 25g	Fat: 15g
Fiber: 7g	Sugar: 12g

STEP BY PREPARATION

- Mix protein powder, almond milk, mixed berries, avocado, flaxseed, and mint leaves in a blender.
- Add ice cubes for a chilled shake, if preferred.
- Blend until smooth and creamy.
- Pour into a glass and enjoy your berry-packed vegan protein shake.

The "Berry Bliss Vegan Shake" is a fusion of health and taste, a smoothie that satisfies your taste buds and nourishes your body. It's a perfect way to enjoy a burst of berry flavors while getting your dose of vegan protein, ensuring you're well-fueled and refreshed for your day's adventures.

Chapter 6 : Antioxidant Infusions

Recipe 31 : Superfood Protein Spectacular Smoothie

Elevate your health with the "Superfood Protein Spectacular Smoothie," a unique blend of high-protein and antioxidant-rich ingredients. This smoothie is a fantastic choice for those looking to boost their nutrient intake while enjoying delicious flavors. Ideal for health enthusiasts and anyone seeking a wellness kick, it combines protein with the power of superfoods, making it perfect for a revitalizing start to the day or a post-workout recovery.

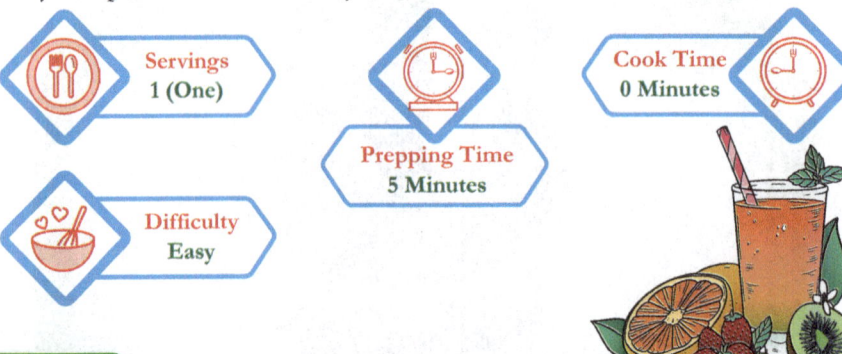

Servings: 1 (One)

Prepping Time: 5 Minutes

Cook Time: 0 Minutes

Difficulty: Easy

INGREDIANT

- ✓ 1 scoop of protein powder (any flavor)
- ✓ 1 cup of unsweetened almond milk
- ✓ 1/2 cup of mixed berries (blueberries, strawberries)
- ✓ 1/4 cup of spinach
- ✓ 1 tbsp of chia seeds
- ✓ 1 tbsp of goji berries
- ✓ 1 tsp of acai powder or matcha
- ✓ Ice cubes (optional)

NUTRITIONAL FACTS: (PER SERVING)

Calories: 300	Protein: 25g
Carbohydrates: 25g	Fat: 8g
Fiber: 6g	Sugar: 10g

STEP BY PREPARATION

- ▷ Add protein powder, almond milk, mixed berries, spinach, chia seeds, goji berries, and acai powder or matcha to a blender.
- ▷ Include ice cubes for a cooler consistency, if desired.
- ▷ Blend until smooth and creamy.
- ▷ Serve in a glass for an immediate nutrient boost.

The "Superfood Protein Spectacular Smoothie" isn't just a drink; it's a celebration of health. Its balanced combination of protein and antioxidants supports your wellness journey, making it a delightful and nourishing addition to your daily routine. Whether you aim for fitness goals or general health, this smoothie is an excellent way to treat your body right.

Chapter 6 : Antioxidant Infusions

Recipe 32 : Antioxidant Protein Power Smoothie

Unleash a wave of wellness with the "Antioxidant Protein Power Smoothie," a blend that perfectly marries high protein with antioxidant-rich ingredients. Ideal for health-conscious individuals, athletes, or anyone looking to boost their nutritional intake, this smoothie is a powerhouse of nourishment. It's an excellent choice for a revitalizing breakfast, a midday pick-me-up, or a post-workout recovery drink, offering a delicious and effective way to support overall health and vitality.

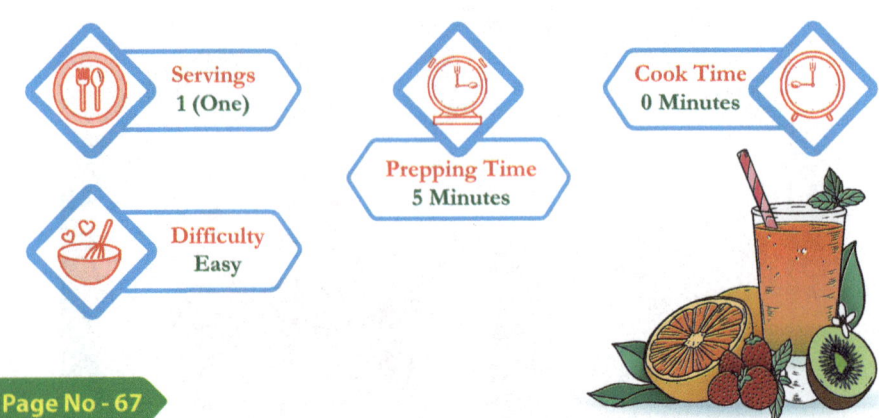

- Servings: 1 (One)
- Prepping Time: 5 Minutes
- Cook Time: 0 Minutes
- Difficulty: Easy

INGREDIANT

- ✅ 1 scoop of your preferred protein powder
- ✅ 1 cup unsweetened almond milk
- ✅ 1/2 cup mixed berries (blueberries, raspberries)
- ✅ 1/4 cup spinach leaves
- ✅ 1 tbsp chia seeds
- ✅ 1 tsp matcha powder
- ✅ A dash of turmeric powder
- ✅ Ice cubes (optional)

NUTRITIONAL FACTS: (PER SERVING)

Calories: 300	Protein: 25g
Carbohydrates: 25g	Fat: 10g
Fiber: 6g	Sugar: 10g

STEP BY PREPARATION

- ▶ Combine protein powder, almond milk, berries, spinach, chia seeds, matcha, and turmeric in a blender.
- ▶ Add ice cubes for a more relaxed texture, if preferred.
- ▶ Blend until smooth and creamy.
- ▶ Pour the smoothie into a glass and relish this nutrient-dense drink.

The "Antioxidant Protein Power Smoothie" is more than just a drink; it's a commitment to your health. It's the perfect way to integrate essential nutrients and antioxidants into your diet while enjoying a delightful and refreshing beverage. Whether seeking to enhance your fitness routine or simply striving for a healthier lifestyle, this smoothie is an excellent choice for staying nourished and energized.

Chapter 6 : Antioxidant Infusions

Recipe 33 : Berry Antioxidant Boost Smoothie

Dive into the refreshing world of the "Berry Antioxidant Boost Smoothie," a delightful fusion of high protein and potent antioxidants. This smoothie is ideal for those looking to nourish their body with essential nutrients while savoring the natural sweetness of berries. Perfect for health enthusiasts, athletes, or anyone seeking a delicious, nutrient-packed beverage, it's great for kickstarting your morning or recharging post-workout.

- **Servings**: 1 (One)
- **Prepping Time**: 5 Minutes
- **Cook Time**: 1 Minutes
- **Difficulty**: Easy

INGREDIANT

- 1 scoop of whey or plant-based protein powder
- 1 cup unsweetened almond milk
- 1/2 cup mixed berries (fresh or frozen)
- 1/4 cup Greek yogurt (or vegan alternative)
- 1 tbsp flaxseed meal
- 1 tsp honey or maple syrup (optional)
- A pinch of cinnamon
- Ice cubes (optional)

NUTRITIONAL FACTS: (PER SERVING)

Calories: 320	Protein: 25g
Carbohydrates: 30g	Fat: 8g
Fiber: 5g	Sugar: 15g

STEP BY PREPARATION

- Blend protein powder, almond milk, mixed berries, Greek yogurt, flaxseed meal, honey/maple syrup, and cinnamon in a blender.
- Add ice cubes for a chilled smoothie, if desired.
- Blend until smooth and creamy.
- Pour into a glass and enjoy your antioxidant-rich protein smoothie.

The "Berry Antioxidant Boost Smoothie" is not just a delicious beverage; it's a powerhouse of nutrition. It's a perfect blend for those who want to maintain a healthy lifestyle while enjoying the delicious flavors of nature. Whether it's a busy morning or a post-exercise refuel, this smoothie offers a convenient and tasty way to support your wellness goals.

Chapter 6 : Antioxidant Infusions

Recipe 34 : Fruit Fusion Protein Blend Smoothie

Embark on a flavorful journey with the "Fruit Fusion Protein Blend Smoothie," a perfect combination of high protein and rich antioxidants. This smoothie is an excellent choice for anyone looking to add a nutritious punch to their diet. Ideal for fitness enthusiasts or those seeking a healthful snack, it blends a variety of fruits with protein power, making it perfect for a revitalizing start to your day or a post-workout refreshment.

Servings: 1 (One)

Prepping Time: 5 Minutes

Cook Time: 0 Minutes

Difficulty: Easy

INGREDIANT

- ✓ 1 scoop of your preferred protein powder
- ✓ 1 cup unsweetened almond milk
- ✓ 1/2 banana
- ✓ 1/4 cup mixed berries
- ✓ 1/4 cup diced mango
- ✓ 1 tbsp chia seeds
- ✓ A splash of orange juice
- ✓ Ice cubes (optional)

NUTRITIONAL FACTS: (PER SERVING)

Calories: 350	Protein: 25g
Carbohydrates: 40g	Fat: 10g
Fiber: 6g	Sugar: 20g

STEP BY PREPARATION

- ▶ Mix protein powder, almond milk, banana, berries, mango, chia seeds, and orange juice in a blender.
- ▶ Add ice cubes for a cooler, thicker smoothie, if preferred.
- ▶ Blend until smooth and creamy.
- ▶ Pour into a glass and savor the fruity, protein-rich smoothie.

The "Fruit Fusion Protein Blend Smoothie" is more than just a drink; it's a vibrant blend of health and taste. It's an ideal way to ensure you're getting a balance of essential nutrients and enjoying a burst of fruit flavors. Whether powering through a workout or looking for a healthy treat, this smoothie is a delicious way to support your wellness journey.

Chapter 6 : Antioxidant Infusions

Recipe 35 : Tropical Antioxidant Treat Smoothie

Escape to a tropical paradise with every sip of the "Tropical Antioxidant Treat Smoothie," a delightful mix combining high protein and a burst of antioxidants. Ideal for those seeking a delicious, health-boosting drink, this smoothie is perfect for fitness enthusiasts, busy professionals, or anyone needing a refreshing, nutrient-rich treat. It's a fantastic choice for an energizing breakfast or a rejuvenating post-workout snack.

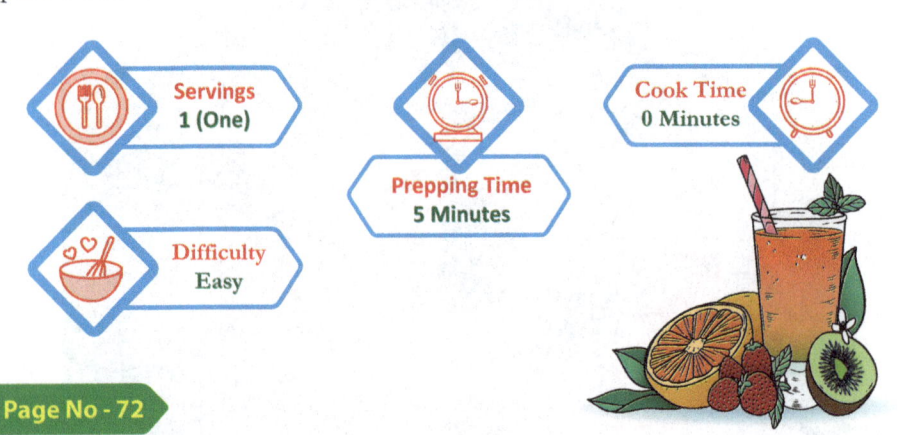

Servings
1 (One)

Prepping Time
5 Minutes

Cook Time
0 Minutes

Difficulty
Easy

Page No - 72

INGREDIANT

- 1 scoop vanilla protein powder
- 1 cup coconut water
- 1/2 cup pineapple chunks
- 1/2 cup mango slices
- 1/4 cup papaya pieces
- 1 tbsp coconut flakes
- A squeeze of lime juice
- Ice cubes (optional)

NUTRITIONAL FACTS: (PER SERVING)

Calories: 350	Protein: 25g
Carbohydrates: 45g	Fat: 5g
Fiber: 5g	Sugar: 30g

STEP BY PREPARATION

Add protein powder, coconut water, pineapple, mango, papaya, coconut flakes, and lime juice to a blender.

Include ice cubes for a chilled smoothie, if desired.

Blend until smooth and creamy.

Serve in a glass and enjoy your tropical smoothie retreat.

The "Tropical Antioxidant Treat Smoothie" is more than a drink; it's a vibrant fusion of flavor and nourishment. Whether you're starting your day or need a midday boost, this smoothie provides a delightful way to infuse your diet with essential proteins and antioxidants, keeping you refreshed and revitalized.

Chapter 6 : Antioxidant Infusions

Recipe 36 : Purple Power Protein Smoothie

Experience a blend of health and taste with the "Purple Power Protein Smoothie," a nutritious concoction that combines high protein with a rich infusion of antioxidants. This smoothie is perfect for anyone seeking a healthful boost, particularly fitness enthusiasts or those needing a nutrient-rich meal replacement. Its vibrant purple hue and delicious flavor make it an excellent choice for a nourishing breakfast or a post-workout replenishment.

- Servings: 1 (One)
- Prepping Time: 5 Minutes
- Cook Time: 0 Minutes
- Difficulty: Easy

INGREDIANT

- 1 scoop of vanilla protein powder
- 1 cup unsweetened almond milk
- 1/2 cup blueberries (fresh or frozen)
- 1/4 cup blackberries
- 1/4 avocado
- 1 tbsp flaxseeds
- A splash of lemon juice
- Ice cubes (optional)

NUTRITIONAL FACTS: (PER SERVING)

Calories: 350	Protein: 25g
Carbohydrates: 30g	Fat: 15g
Fiber: 8g	Sugar: 15g

STEP BY PREPARATION

- Combine protein powder, almond milk, blueberries, blackberries, avocado, flaxseeds, and lemon juice in a blender.
- Add ice cubes for a chilled texture, if desired.
- Blend until smooth and creamy.
- Pour into a glass and enjoy the energizing, antioxidant-packed smoothie.

The "Purple Power Protein Smoothie" is not just a beverage; it's a healthful journey. It's the perfect way to fuel your body with essential nutrients and antioxidants while indulging in a deliciously sweet and satisfying treat. Whether starting your day or needing a midday boost, this smoothie is an excellent choice for maintaining a balanced and healthy lifestyle.

Chapter 7 : Dessert-Inspired Delights

Recipe 37 : Chocolate Peanut Butter Dream Smoothie

Indulge in the decadent Chocolate Peanut Butter Dream Smoothie, a high-protein treat that mirrors the flavors of your favorite dessert. This smoothie is perfect for those who crave a sweet treat but still want to maintain a healthy lifestyle. It combines the irresistible flavors of chocolate and peanut butter in a nutritious, protein-rich beverage, ideal for fitness enthusiasts or anyone with a sweet tooth.

Servings
1 (One)

Prepping Time
5 Minutes

Cook Time
0 Minutes

Difficulty
Easy

INGREDIANT

- ✅ 1 scoop of chocolate protein powder
- ✅ 1 cup almond milk
- ✅ 2 tbsp natural peanut butter
- ✅ 1/2 ripe banana
- ✅ 1 tbsp cocoa powder
- ✅ 1 tsp honey or maple syrup (optional)
- ✅ Ice cubes (optional)

NUTRITIONAL FACTS: (PER SERVING)

Calories: 400	Protein: 30g
Carbohydrates: 30g	Fat: 20g
Fiber: 5g	Sugar: 15g

STEP BY PREPARATION

- ▶ In a blender, combine protein powder, almond milk, peanut butter, banana, cocoa powder, and honey/maple syrup.
- ▶ Add ice cubes for a thicker consistency, if preferred.
- ▶ Blend until smooth and creamy.
- ▶ Serve in a glass and savor your chocolate peanut butter delight.

The "Chocolate Peanut Butter Dream Smoothie" is not just a beverage; it's a guilt-free escape into dessert heaven. Whether you need a post-workout reward or a healthy snack alternative, this smoothie offers the perfect balance of taste and nutrition, making it a delightful choice for any time of the day.

Chapter 7 : Dessert-Inspired Delights

Recipe 38 : Strawberry Cheesecake Protein Shake Smoothie

Savor the essence of dessert with a healthy twist in the Strawberry Cheesecake Protein Shake, a high-protein smoothie inspired by the classic dessert. This smoothie blends the luscious flavors of strawberries and cheesecake into a nutritious, protein-packed drink, perfect for those with a sweet tooth and fitness goals. It's ideal for a post-workout treat, a delicious breakfast, or a satisfying snack.

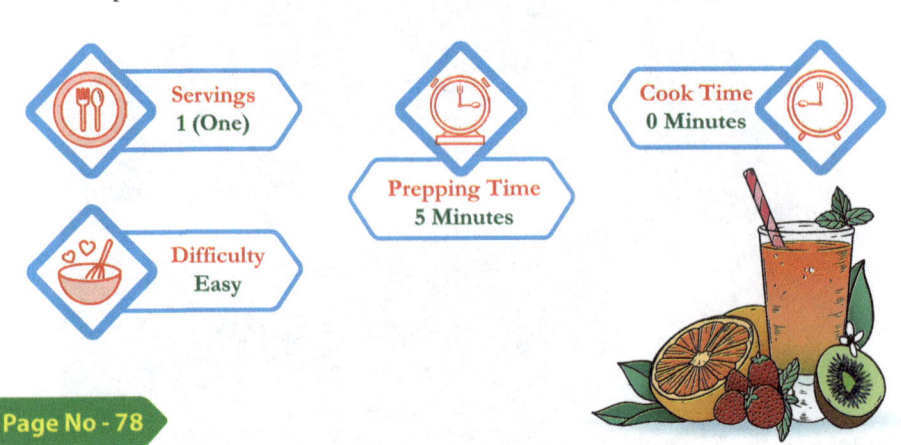

Servings: 1 (One)

Prepping Time: 5 Minutes

Cook Time: 0 Minutes

Difficulty: Easy

INGREDIANT

- ✅ 1 scoop vanilla protein powder
- ✅ 1 cup unsweetened almond milk
- ✅ 1/2 cup frozen strawberries
- ✅ 1/4 cup Greek yogurt (or vegan alternative)
- ✅ 2 tbsp low-fat cream cheese (or vegan alternative)
- ✅ 1 tsp honey or agave syrup
- ✅ A dash of vanilla extract
- ✅ Ice cubes (optional)

NUTRITIONAL FACTS: (PER SERVING)

Calories: 350	Protein: 30g
Carbohydrates: 25g	Fat: 10g
Fiber: 4g	Sugar: 15g

STEP BY PREPARATION

- ▶ Blend protein powder, almond milk, strawberries, Greek yogurt, cream cheese, honey/agave syrup, and vanilla extract in a blender.
- ▶ Add ice cubes for a chilled and thicker smoothie, if desired.
- ▶ Blend until smooth and creamy. Pour into a glass and enjoy your strawberry cheesecake indulgence.

The "Strawberry Cheesecake Protein Shake" isn't just a smoothie; it's a delightful fusion of indulgence and nutrition. Whether you're refueling after a workout or seeking a healthy alternative to satisfy your dessert cravings, this smoothie is an intelligent choice, blending the joy of dessert with the benefits of a protein shake.

Chapter 7 : Dessert-Inspired Delights

Recipe 39 : Vanilla Almond Indulgence Smoothie

Indulge in the delightful Vanilla Almond Indulgence Smoothie, a luxurious blend that marries the richness of vanilla and almonds in a high-protein treat. This smoothie is perfect for those who enjoy the finer flavors while keeping an eye on their nutritional goals. It's ideal for a sumptuous post-workout recovery, a luxurious breakfast, or a satisfying, healthful snack, offering exquisite taste and nutritional benefits.

- Servings: 1 (One)
- Prepping Time: 5 Minutes
- Cook Time: 0 Minutes
- Difficulty: Easy

INGREDIANT

- 1 scoop vanilla protein powder
- 1 cup unsweetened almond milk
- 2 tbsp almond butter
- 1/2 banana, frozen
- A dash of cinnamon
- 1 tsp honey or maple syrup (optional)
- A few drops of almond extract (optional)
- Ice cubes (optional)

NUTRITIONAL FACTS: (PER SERVING)

Calories: 400	Protein: 30g
Carbohydrates: 30g	Fat: 20g
Fiber: 5g	Sugar: 15g

STEP BY PREPARATION

- In a blender, combine protein powder, almond milk, almond butter, banana, cinnamon, honey/maple syrup, and almond extract.
- Add ice cubes for a thicker consistency, if desired.
- Blend until smooth and creamy.
- Pour into a glass and savor the creamy, nutty richness.

The "Vanilla Almond Indulgence Smoothie" is not just a drink; it's a celebration of flavors. Perfect for those seeking a luxurious twist on their protein intake, this smoothie combines the comforting flavors of vanilla and almond in a nourishing and satisfying way, making it an excellent addition to your daily routine.

Chapter 7 : Dessert-Inspired Delights

Recipe 40 : Banana Split Protein Blend Smoothie

Indulge in the guilt-free pleasure of the "Banana Split Protein Blend Smoothie," a delightful twist on the classic dessert. This high-protein smoothie is perfect for those craving a sweet treat while prioritizing their health and fitness goals. Combining the decadent flavors of a banana split with nutritious ingredients, it's ideal for a post-workout boost, a satisfying breakfast, or a healthy snack.

Servings: 1 (One)

Prepping Time: 5 Minutes

Cook Time: 0 Minutes

Difficulty: Easy

INGREDIANT

- ✓ 1 scoop vanilla protein powder
- ✓ 1 cup unsweetened almond milk
- ✓ 1 ripe banana
- ✓ 2 strawberries, sliced
- ✓ 1 tbsp unsweetened cocoa powder
- ✓ 1 tbsp chopped nuts (almonds or walnuts)
- ✓ A drizzle of honey or maple syrup
- ✓ A sprinkle of shredded coconut (optional)
- ✓ Ice cubes (optional)

NUTRITIONAL FACTS: (PER SERVING)

Calories: 350	Protein: 25g
Carbohydrates: 40g	Fat: 10g
Fiber: 5g	Sugar: 20g

STEP BY PREPARATION

- ▷ Add protein powder, almond milk, banana, strawberries, cocoa powder, nuts, honey/maple syrup, and shredded coconut to a blender.
- ▷ Include ice cubes for a thicker smoothie, if preferred.
- ▷ Blend until smooth and creamy.
- ▷ Pour into a glass and enjoy your banana split in a cup.

The "Banana Split Protein Blend Smoothie" is more than just a beverage; it's a creative and nutritious way to enjoy the flavors of your favorite dessert. Whether you're fueling up after a workout or looking for a delicious and healthy treat, this smoothie offers a perfect blend of taste and nutrition, making it a delightful addition to your daily routine.

Chapter 7 : Dessert-Inspired Delights

Recipe 41 : Caramel Apple Protein Twist Smoothie

Embark on a delightful culinary journey with the "Caramel Apple Protein Twist Smoothie," a high-protein treat that brings the classic flavors of a caramel apple to your glass. This smoothie is perfect for those seeking a delicious, dessert-inspired protein boost. Ideal for post-workout recovery, a nutritious breakfast, or a satisfying snack, it combines the sweet taste of caramel apples with the benefits of a protein shake.

Servings
1 (One)

Prepping Time
5 Minutes

Cook Time
0 Minutes

Difficulty
Easy

INGREDIANT

- ✅ 1 scoop vanilla protein powder
- ✅ 1 cup unsweetened almond milk
- ✅ 1 small apple, chopped
- ✅ 2 tbsp Greek yogurt (or vegan alternative)
- ✅ 1 tbsp caramel sauce (or to taste)
- ✅ A pinch of cinnamon
- ✅ Ice cubes (optional)

NUTRITIONAL FACTS: (PER SERVING)

Calories: 350	Protein: 25g
Carbohydrates: 45g	Fat: 8g
Fiber: 4g	Sugar: 30g

STEP BY PREPARATION

- ▶ Blend protein powder, almond milk, apple, Greek yogurt, caramel sauce, and cinnamon in a blender.
- ▶ Add ice cubes for a chilled texture, if desired.
- ▶ Blend until smooth and creamy.
- ▶ Serve in a glass and enjoy the fusion of caramel apple delight.

The "Caramel Apple Protein Twist Smoothie" is not just a drink; it's a novel way to enjoy your favorite flavors in a healthy, protein-rich form. Whether you're a fitness enthusiast or simply looking for a tasty yet nutritious treat, this smoothie offers a delightful blend of taste, health, and satisfaction.

Chapter 7 : Dessert-Inspired Delights

Recipe 42 : Protein Packed Pina Colada Smoothie

Escape to a tropical paradise with the "Protein Packed Piña Colada Smoothie," a delightful twist on the classic beachside drink. This high-protein smoothie is perfect for those who crave a sweet, tropical treat while staying on track with their health and fitness goals. Ideal as a post-workout refreshment or a nutrient-rich snack, it brings the flavors of a vacation into your daily routine.

Servings: 1 (One)
Prepping Time: 5 Minutes
Cook Time: 0 Minutes
Difficulty: Easy

INGREDIANT

- 1 scoop vanilla protein powder
- 1 cup unsweetened coconut milk
- 1/2 cup frozen pineapple chunks
- 1/4 cup Greek yogurt (or vegan alternative)
- 1 tbsp shredded coconut
- A splash of pineapple juice (optional)
- Ice cubes (optional)

NUTRITIONAL FACTS: (PER SERVING)

Calories: 350	Protein: 25g
Carbohydrates: 35g	Fat: 10g
Fiber: 3g	Sugar: 25g

STEP BY PREPARATION

- Blend protein powder, coconut milk, pineapple chunks, Greek yogurt, shredded coconut, and pineapple juice in a blender.
- Add ice cubes for a cooler, thicker smoothie, if preferred.
- Blend until smooth and creamy.
- Pour into a glass and enjoy your protein-rich tropical treat.

The "Protein Packed Piña Colada Smoothie" is more than just a beverage; it's a healthy indulgence. Whether you're looking for a delicious way to boost your protein intake or simply dreaming of a tropical getaway, this smoothie is a perfect choice, combining the joy of a classic dessert with the benefits of a protein shake.

Chapter 8 : Energy-Boosting Blends

Recipe 43 : Energizer Espresso Protein Smoothie

Energize your day with the Energizer Espresso Protein Smoothie, a dynamic fusion of high protein and invigorating espresso. This smoothie is perfect for coffee lovers and fitness enthusiasts, offering a delicious way to combine a caffeine kick with muscle-building protein. Ideal for a morning start, a midday boost, or a post-workout pick-me-up, it's a tasty and effective way to energize both body and mind.

Servings: 1 (One)
Prepping Time: 5 Minutes
Cook Time: 0 Minutes
Difficulty: Easy

INGREDIANT

- ✅ 1 scoop chocolate or vanilla protein powder
- ✅ 1 shot of espresso or 1/2 cup strong brewed coffee, cooled
- ✅ 1 cup almond milk
- ✅ 1/2 banana, frozen
- ✅ 1 tbsp almond butter
- ✅ A pinch of cinnamon
- ✅ Ice cubes (optional)

NUTRITIONAL FACTS: (PER SERVING)

Calories: 350	Protein: 25g
Carbohydrates: 30g	Fat: 15g
Fiber: 4g	Sugar: 15g

STEP BY PREPARATION

- ▶ Blend protein powder, espresso/coffee, almond milk, banana, almond butter, and cinnamon in a blender.
- ▶ Add ice cubes for a chilled smoothie, if preferred.
- ▶ Blend until smooth and creamy.
- ▶ Pour into a glass and enjoy the energizing blend.

The "Energizer Espresso Protein Smoothie" is more than just a beverage; it's a powerhouse of energy and nutrition. Whether you're gearing up for a workout or need a lift during a busy day, this smoothie offers the perfect balance of taste and energy, helping you stay active and focused.

Chapter 8 : Energy-Boosting Blends

Recipe 44 : Citrus Energy Zing Smoothie

Revitalize your senses with the "Citrus Energy Zing Smoothie," a zesty and refreshing high-protein blend. This smoothie is a perfect pick-me-up, combining the refreshing taste of citrus with a protein punch to fuel your day. Whether you're kickstarting your morning, seeking a midday energy boost, or needing post-workout nourishment, this bright and lively smoothie is an excellent choice for a healthy,

Servings 1 (One)

Prepping Time 5 Minutes

Cook Time 0 Minutes

Difficulty Easy

INGREDIANT

- ✅ 1 scoop vanilla protein powder
- ✅ 1 cup orange juice, freshly squeezed
- ✅ 1/2 grapefruit, juiced
- ✅ 1/4 lemon, juiced
- ✅ 1/2 banana, frozen
- ✅ 1 tbsp Greek yogurt (or vegan alternative)
- ✅ A sprinkle of grated ginger

NUTRITIONAL FACTS: (PER SERVING)

Calories: 350	Protein: 25g
Carbohydrates: 45g	Fat: 5g
Fiber: 3g	Sugar: 30g

STEP BY PREPARATION

- ▶ Mix protein powder, orange, grapefruit, lemon, banana, Greek yogurt, and ginger in a blender.
- ▶ Add ice cubes for extra chill, if desired.
- ▶ Blend until smooth and frothy.
- ▶ Serve in a glass and experience the refreshing energy boost.

The "Citrus Energy Zing Smoothie" isn't just a drink; it's an explosion of flavor and energy. It's an ideal way to incorporate a burst of natural vitamins and protein into your diet, ensuring you stay refreshed, energized, and ready to tackle your day with zest.

Chapter 8 : Energy-Boosting Blends

Recipe 45 : Tropical Morning Motivator Smoothie

Begin your day with the "Tropical Morning Motivator Smoothie," a vibrant and energetic high-protein blend that captures the essence of tropical flavors. This smoothie is an excellent choice for those seeking a delicious, energizing start to their day. Perfect for busy mornings, post-workout recovery, or a midday energy boost, it combines the zest of tropical fruits with protein to keep you fueled and focused.

Servings
1 (One)

Prepping Time
5 Minutes

Cook Time
0 Minutes

Difficulty
Easy

INGREDIANT

- ✅ 1 scoop vanilla protein powder
- ✅ 1 cup coconut water
- ✅ 1/2 cup pineapple chunks
- ✅ 1/2 mango, diced
- ✅ 1/4 banana, frozen
- ✅ 1 tbsp chia seeds
- ✅ A splash of lime juice
- ✅ Ice cubes (optional)

NUTRITIONAL FACTS: (PER SERVING)

Calories: 350	Protein: 25g
Carbohydrates: 45g	Fat: 5g
Fiber: 5g	Sugar: 30g

STEP BY PREPARATION

- ▶ In a blender, combine protein powder, coconut water, pineapple, mango, banana, chia seeds, and lime juice.
- ▶ Add ice cubes for a chilled smoothie, if preferred.
- ▶ Blend until smooth and creamy.
- ▶ Pour into a glass and embrace the tropical energy.

The "Tropical Morning Motivator Smoothie" is more than just a drink; it's a refreshing way to start your day with energy and flavor. Whether you're gearing up for a workout or need a nutritious breakfast, this smoothie is the perfect blend of taste, health, and motivation.

Chapter 8 : Energy-Boosting Blends

Recipe 46 : Mango Tango Energy Shake Smoothie

Step into a world of flavor and energy with the "Mango Tango Energy Shake Smoothie," a high-protein, energizing beverage perfect for rejuvenating your body and mind. This smoothie is ideal for those needing an extra boost, combining the sweet, tropical taste of mango with a protein kick. It's great for jump-starting your day, fueling up pre-workout, or recharging post-exercise.

- Servings: 1 (One)
- Prepping Time: 5 Minutes
- Cook Time: 0 Minutes
- Difficulty: Easy

INGREDIANT

- ✅ 1 scoop vanilla protein powder
- ✅ 1 cup almond milk
- ✅ 1 ripe mango, diced
- ✅ 1/2 banana, frozen
- ✅ 1 tbsp Greek yogurt (or vegan alternative)
- ✅ A pinch of ground turmeric
- ✅ Ice cubes (optional)

NUTRITIONAL FACTS: (PER SERVING)

Calories: 350	Protein: 25g
Carbohydrates: 50g	Fat: 5g
Fiber: 5g	Sugar: 35g

STEP BY PREPARATION

- ▶ Blend protein powder, almond milk, mango, banana, Greek yogurt, and turmeric in a blender.
- ▶ Add ice cubes for a colder, thicker shake, if desired.
- ▶ Blend until smooth and creamy.
- ▶ Serve in a glass and enjoy the tropical, energetic delight.

The "Mango Tango Energy Shake Smoothie" is more than just a tasty beverage; it's a delightful way to infuse your day with energy and nutrition. Perfect for those on the go, it provides a convenient and delicious method to ensure you're powered up and ready to face whatever the day brings.

Chapter 8 : Energy-Boosting Blends

Recipe 47 : Berry Blast Power Smoothie

Embark on a flavorful journey with the "Berry Blast Power Smoothie," a high-protein, energy-boosting delight perfect for rejuvenating your body. Ideal for active individuals or anyone needing a nutritious pick-me-up, this smoothie blends a variety of berries with protein power, providing a delicious and effective way to start your day or recharge after a workout.

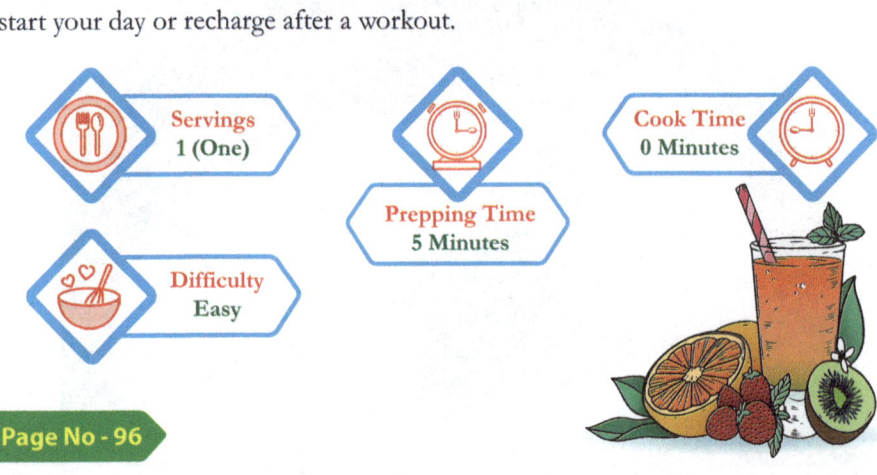

Servings: 1 (One)

Prepping Time: 5 Minutes

Cook Time: 0 Minutes

Difficulty: Easy

INGREDIANT

- 1 scoop protein powder (flavor of choice)
- 1 cup almond milk
- 1/2 cup mixed berries (blueberries, strawberries, raspberries)
- 1/4 banana, frozen
- 1 tbsp chia seeds
- A dash of honey or maple syrup (optional)
- Ice cubes (optional)

NUTRITIONAL FACTS: (PER SERVING)

Calories: 300	Protein: 25g
Carbohydrates: 30g	Fat: 5g
Fiber: 6g	Sugar: 15g

STEP BY PREPARATION

- Mix a blender with protein powder, almond milk, berries, banana, chia seeds, and honey/maple syrup.
- Add ice cubes for a thicker consistency, if desired.
- Blend until smooth and creamy.
- Pour into a glass and savor the berry-infused energy boost.

The "Berry Blast Power Smoothie" is more than just a drink; it's a vibrant blend of taste and energy. Whether you're seeking a morning energy boost or a post-exercise recharge, this smoothie offers a delicious, healthful way to energize and satisfy, helping you tackle your day with renewed vigor.

Chapter 8 : Energy-Boosting Blends

Recipe 48 : Green Tea Energy Infusion Smoothie

Introducing the "Green Tea Energy Infusion Smoothie," a unique blend that combines the rejuvenating properties of green tea with high protein for a powerful energy boost. This smoothie is ideal for those seeking a natural lift to their day. Perfect for busy mornings, pre-workout energizing, or a midday pick-me-up, it's a refreshing way to integrate health and vitality into your routine.

Servings: 1 (One)

Prepping Time: 5 Minutes

Cook Time: 0 Minutes

Difficulty: Easy

INGREDIANT

- 1 scoop vanilla protein powder
- 1 cup brewed green tea, cooled
- 1/2 cup spinach leaves
- 1/4 ripe avocado
- 1 tbsp honey or agave nectar
- A squeeze of lemon juice
- Ice cubes (optional)

NUTRITIONAL FACTS: (PER SERVING)

Calories: 250	Protein: 20g
Carbohydrates: 20g	Fat: 10g
Fiber: 4g	Sugar: 10g

STEP BY PREPARATION

- Place protein powder, green tea, spinach, avocado, honey/agave, and lemon juice in a blender.
- Add ice cubes for a chilled smoothie, if preferred.
- Blend until smooth and consistent.
- Pour into a glass and enjoy your energizing green tea concoction.

The "Green Tea Energy Infusion Smoothie" is more than just a beverage; it's a fusion of wellness and energy. Whether you're starting your day or need a boost, this smoothie provides a delicious and healthful way to energize and refresh, helping you tackle your daily activities with renewed zest and vitality.

Chapter 9 : Nut Butter Nourishers

Recipe 49 : Peanut Butter Power Smoothie

Delight in the creamy goodness of the "Peanut Butter Power Smoothie," a rich and satisfying blend that's a favorite among high-protein nut butter enthusiasts. This smoothie is a fantastic choice for those who love the hearty flavor of peanut butter combined with the benefits of protein. It's perfect for a fulfilling breakfast, a replenishing post-workout drink, or a nutritious snack to energize you throughout the day

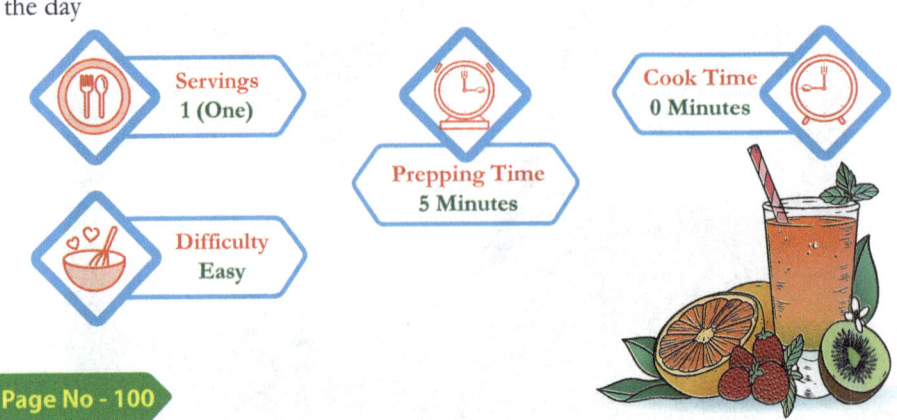

- **Servings**: 1 (One)
- **Prepping Time**: 5 Minutes
- **Cook Time**: 0 Minutes
- **Difficulty**: Easy

INGREDIANT

- ✓ 1 scoop chocolate or vanilla protein powder
- ✓ 1 cup almond milk
- ✓ 2 tbsp natural peanut butter
- ✓ 1/2 banana, frozen
- ✓ 1 tbsp oats
- ✓ A pinch of cinnamon
- ✓ Ice cubes (optional)

NUTRITIONAL FACTS: (PER SERVING)

Calories: 400	Protein: 30g
Carbohydrates: 35g	Fat: 15g
Fiber: 5g	Sugar: 15g

STEP BY PREPARATION

- ▶ Blend protein powder, almond milk, peanut butter, banana, oats, and cinnamon in a blender.
- ▶ Add ice cubes for a thicker texture, if preferred.
- ▶ Blend until smooth and creamy.
- ▶ Serve in a glass and enjoy the nutty, protein-packed smoothie.

The "Peanut Butter Power Smoothie" is more than just a tasty drink; it's a nutritional powerhouse. Whether you're looking for a quick breakfast option, a post-exercise recovery drink, or a satisfying snack, this smoothie is a delicious way to incorporate healthy fats and protein into your diet, keeping you full and energized.

Chapter 9 : Nut Butter Nourishers

Recipe 50 : Almond Joy Protein Shake Smoothie

Indulge in the delightful "Almond Joy Protein Shake Smoothie," where the classic candy bar meets nutritious ingredients. This high-protein smoothie is a treat for those who adore the combination of almonds, coconut, and chocolate, all while keeping health in mind. It's excellent for a decadent breakfast, a satisfying post-workout refuel, or a delightful snack that offers pleasure and nourishment.

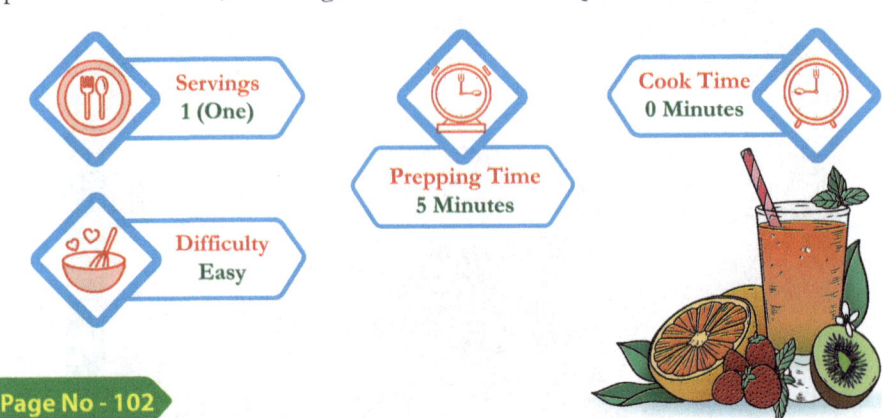

- Servings: 1 (One)
- Prepping Time: 5 Minutes
- Cook Time: 0 Minutes
- Difficulty: Easy

INGREDIANT

- ✅ 1 scoop of chocolate protein powder
- ✅ 1 cup unsweetened almond milk
- ✅ 2 tbsp unsweetened shredded coconut
- ✅ 1 tbsp almond butter
- ✅ 1/4 tsp coconut extract (optional)
- ✅ A few dark chocolate chips (for garnish)
- ✅ Ice cubes (optional)

NUTRITIONAL FACTS: (PER SERVING)

Calories: 350	Protein: 25g
Carbohydrates: 25g	Fat: 15g
Fiber: 5g	Sugar: 10g

STEP BY PREPARATION

- ▶ Combine protein powder, almond milk, shredded coconut, almond butter, and coconut extract in a blender.
- ▶ Add ice cubes for a colder and thicker shake, if desired.
- ▶ Blend until smooth and creamy.
- ▶ Garnish with a few chocolate chips.
- ▶ Serve in a glass and relish the
- ▶ flavors of an Almond Joy in a healthy shake.

The "Almond Joy Protein Shake Smoothie" is more than a mere smoothie; it's a delightful fusion of flavor and nutrition. Perfect for satisfying your sweet cravings while fueling your body with protein and healthy fats, this smoothie proves that you can enjoy the flavors you love nourishing and healthfully.

Chapter 9 : Nut Butter Nourishers

Recipe 51 : Cashew Cream Dream Smoothie

Dive into the creamy bliss of the "Cashew Cream Dream Smoothie," a luxurious and nourishing concoction for nut butter lovers. This high-protein smoothie blends the rich, smooth taste of cashews into a dreamy beverage. Perfect for those seeking a decadent yet healthy treat, it's ideal for a sumptuous breakfast, a rejuvenating post-workout drink, or a satisfying snack that combines indulgence with nutrition.

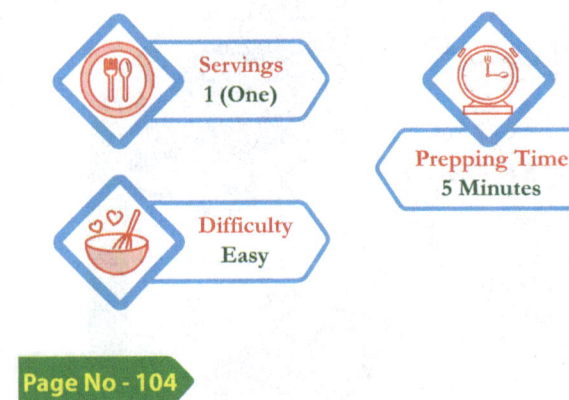

- **Servings**: 1 (One)
- **Prepping Time**: 5 Minutes
- **Cook Time**: 0 Minutes
- **Difficulty**: Easy

INGREDIANT

- ✓ 1 scoop vanilla protein powder
- ✓ 1 cup almond milk
- ✓ 2 tbsp cashew butter
- ✓ 1/2 banana, frozen
- ✓ 1 tbsp honey or agave syrup
- ✓ A pinch of cinnamon
- ✓ Ice cubes (optional)

NUTRITIONAL FACTS: (PER SERVING)

Calories: 400	Protein: 30g
Carbohydrates: 35g	Fat: 18g
Fiber: 4g	Sugar: 20g

STEP BY PREPARATION

- ▶ Mix protein powder, almond milk, cashew butter, banana, honey/agave syrup, and cinnamon in a blender.
- ▶ Include ice cubes for a thicker consistency, if desired.
- ▶ Blend until smooth and creamy.
- ▶ Pour into a glass and enjoy the rich, nutty flavor.

The "Cashew Cream Dream Smoothie" is more than just a beverage; it's a delightful escape into a world of creamy nuttiness. Whether looking for a luxurious way to start your day or a healthy snack to satiate your cravings, this smoothie offers the perfect blend of taste and nutrition, making it an excellent addition to your daily routine.

Chapter 9 : Nut Butter Nourishers

Recipe 52 : Nutty Banana Protein Boost Smoothie

Discover the delightful fusion of flavors in the "Nutty Banana Protein Boost Smoothie," a creamy, high-protein beverage perfect for nut butter enthusiasts. This smoothie combines the comforting taste of bananas with a decadent nut butter twist, making it ideal for a nutritious breakfast, a post-workout replenishment, or a satisfying snack. It's a beautiful choice for those seeking a healthful yet delicious protein-packed treat.

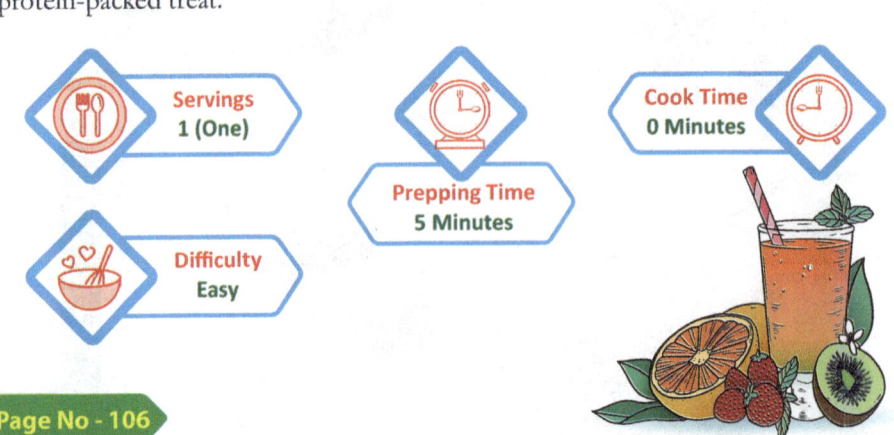

- **Servings:** 1 (One)
- **Prepping Time:** 5 Minutes
- **Cook Time:** 0 Minutes
- **Difficulty:** Easy

INGREDIANT

- 1 scoop vanilla protein powder
- 1 cup almond milk
- 1 ripe banana
- 2 tbsp peanut or almond butter
- 1 tbsp flaxseed meal
- A dash of cinnamon
- Ice cubes (optional)

NUTRITIONAL FACTS: (PER SERVING)

Calories: 400	Protein: 30g
Carbohydrates: 40g	Fat: 15g
Fiber: 5g	Sugar: 20g

STEP BY PREPARATION

- Blend protein powder, almond milk, banana, nut butter, flaxseed meal, and cinnamon in a blender.
- Add ice cubes for a cooler, thicker shake, if preferred.
- Blend until smooth and creamy.
- Pour into a glass and enjoy the nutty, banana-infused protein boost.

The "Nutty Banana Protein Boost Smoothie" is more than a drink; it's a satisfying blend of nutrition and flavor. Whether you're a fitness enthusiast or just looking for a healthy alternative to satisfy your cravings, this smoothie offers a delicious way to incorporate protein and essential nutrients into your diet, ensuring you stay energized and fulfilled.

Chapter 9 : Nut Butter Nourishers

Recipe 53 : Hazelnut Heaven Smoothie

Step into a world of indulgence with the "Hazelnut Heaven Smoothie," a luxurious and creamy high-protein drink for all nut butter lovers. This smoothie perfectly blends the rich, irresistible flavor of hazelnuts with the nutritional benefits of protein, creating a divine experience. Ideal for a decadent breakfast, a fulfilling post-workout treat, or a delightful snack, it offers a sumptuous way to fuel your day while satisfying your taste buds.

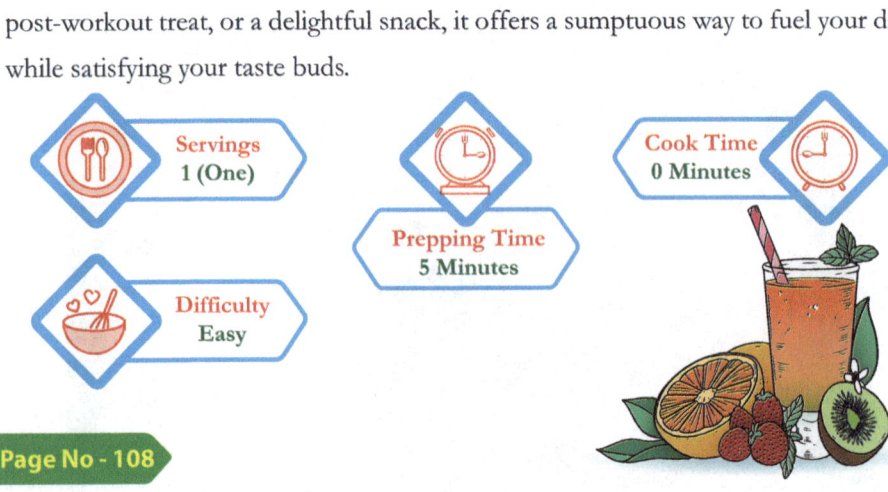

- Servings: 1 (One)
- Prepping Time: 5 Minutes
- Cook Time: 0 Minutes
- Difficulty: Easy

INGREDIANT

- ✓ 1 scoop of chocolate protein powder
- ✓ 1 cup almond milk
- ✓ 2 tbsp hazelnut butter
- ✓ 1/2 banana, frozen
- ✓ 1 tbsp cocoa powder
- ✓ A drizzle of honey or maple syrup (optional)
- ✓ Ice cubes (optional)

NUTRITIONAL FACTS: (PER SERVING)

Calories: 400	Protein: 25g
Carbohydrates: 35g	Fat: 20g
Fiber: 6g	Sugar: 15g

STEP BY PREPARATION

- ▶ Blend protein powder, almond milk, hazelnut butter, banana, and cocoa powder in a blender.
- ▶ Add honey/maple syrup for sweetness, if desired.
- ▶ Include ice cubes for a thicker consistency, if preferred.
- ▶ Blend until smooth and creamy.
- ▶ Serve in a glass and savor the heavenly hazelnut flavor.

The "Hazelnut Heaven Smoothie" is not just a beverage; it's an exquisite blend of taste and nutrition. Perfect for those seeking a luxurious twist on their protein intake, this smoothie combines the comforting flavors of hazelnut and chocolate in a nourishing and satisfying way, making it an excellent addition to your daily routine.

Chapter 9 : Nut Butter Nourishers

Recipe 54 : Pecan Pie Protein Treat Smoothie

Savor the classic flavors of a favorite dessert with the "Pecan Pie Protein Treat Smoothie," a delightful high-protein smoothie that brings the essence of pecan pie to your glass. Ideal for those who adore nutty sweetness and seek nutritional benefits, this smoothie is perfect for a comforting breakfast, a luxurious post-workout treat, or a satisfying snack that marries indulgence with health.

Servings: 1 (One)
Prepping Time: 5 Minutes
Cook Time: 0 Minutes
Difficulty: Easy

INGREDIANT

- ✓ 1 scoop vanilla protein powder
- ✓ 1 cup almond milk
- ✓ 2 tbsp pecan butter (or crushed pecans)
- ✓ 1/2 banana, frozen
- ✓ A pinch of cinnamon
- ✓ A drizzle of maple syrup
- ✓ Ice cubes (optional)

NUTRITIONAL FACTS: (PER SERVING)

Calories: 350	Protein: 25g
Carbohydrates: 30g	Fat: 15g
Fiber: 4g	Sugar: 20g

STEP BY PREPARATION

- ▶ In a blender, combine protein powder, almond milk, pecan butter/crushed pecans, banana, cinnamon, and maple syrup.
- ▶ Add ice cubes for a thicker smoothie, if desired.
- ▶ Blend until smooth and creamy.
- ▶ Pour into a glass and enjoy your pecan pie in a healthy, protein-rich form.

The "Pecan Pie Protein Treat Smoothie" is more than just a smoothie; it's a delightful and nutritious escape. Whether you're longing for a slice of pecan pie or need a healthy snack, this smoothie offers a perfect balance of taste and health, making it an excellent addition to your daily routine.

Chapter 1 : Night-Time Nurturers

Recipe 55 : Sweet Dreams Protein Shake Smoothie

Embrace the tranquility of the evening with the "Sweet Dreams Protein Shake Smoothie," designed to nurture your body with high protein as night falls. This soothing smoothie is perfect for those who seek a comforting, sleep-friendly snack. It combines gentle, calming ingredients with protein to support overnight muscle recovery, making it ideal for a pre-sleep ritual or a relaxing end to a busy day.

- Servings: 1 (One)
- Prepping Time: 5 Minutes
- Cook Time: 0 Minutes
- Difficulty: Easy

INGREDIANT

- 1 scoop of casein or slow-digesting protein powder
- 1 cup almond milk or milk of choice
- 1/2 banana
- 1 tbsp almond butter
- A sprinkle of nutmeg or cinnamon
- A dash of vanilla extract
- Ice cubes (optional)

NUTRITIONAL FACTS: (PER SERVING)

Calories: 350	Protein: 25g
Carbohydrates: 25g	Fat: 10g
Fiber: 4g	Sugar: 10g

STEP BY PREPARATION

- Blend protein powder, milk, banana, almond butter, nutmeg/cinnamon, and vanilla extract in a blender.
- Add ice cubes for a more excellent smoothie, if desired.
- Blend until smooth and creamy.
- Serve in a glass and relax into your evening.

The "Sweet Dreams Protein Shake Smoothie" is more than just a nighttime drink; it's a comforting embrace for your body and mind. Ideal for those winding down after a day's activities, it offers a delicious way to nourish your body while preparing for a restful night's sleep.

Chapter 1 : Night-Time Nurturers

Recipe 56 : Moonlight Cherry Almond Smoothie

Experience the calming blend of the "Moonlight Cherry Almond Smoothie," a high-protein, night-time nurturer designed to soothe and satisfy. Ideal for those seeking a peaceful evening treat, this smoothie combines the sweetness of cherries with the nuttiness of almonds, all while providing protein benefits to support overnight recovery. It's perfect as a pre-bedtime snack or a relaxing way to end your day.

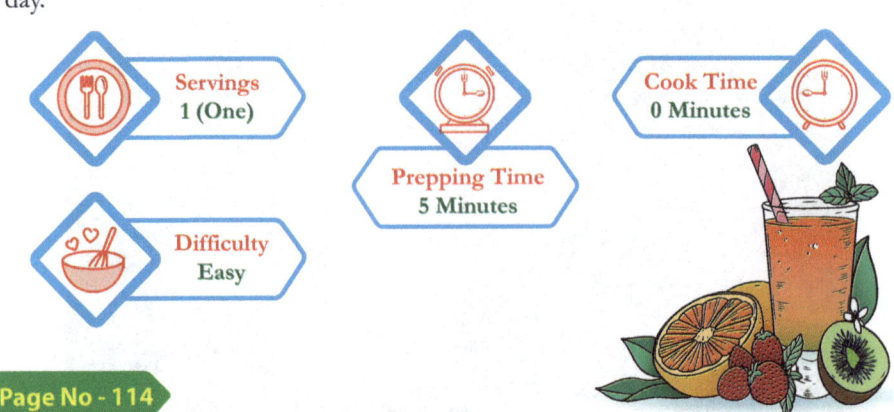

Servings 1 (One)

Prepping Time 5 Minutes

Cook Time 0 Minutes

Difficulty Easy

INGREDIANT

- ✓ 1 scoop vanilla or cherry-flavored
- ✓ protein powder
- ✓ 1 cup almond milk
- ✓ 1/2 cup frozen cherries
- ✓ 2 tbsp almond butter
- ✓ A dash of cinnamon
- ✓ A few drops of almond extract
- ✓ (optional)
- ✓ Ice cubes (optional)

NUTRITIONAL FACTS: (PER SERVING)

Calories: 350	Protein: 25g
Carbohydrates: 30g	Fat: 15g
Fiber: 5g	Sugar: 20g

STEP BY PREPARATION

▶ Place protein powder, almond milk, cherries, almond butter, cinnamon, and almond extract in a blender.

▶ Add ice cubes for a chilled texture, if preferred.

▶ Blend until smooth and creamy.

▶ Pour into a glass and enjoy the serene cherry almond flavor.

The "Moonlight Cherry Almond Smoothie" is more than just a drink; it's a nightly ritual to nurture your body and soul. Whether you're looking to unwind after a long day or need a satisfying, healthy snack before bed, this smoothie offers a perfect combination of taste and tranquility, ensuring a restful and rejuvenating night.

Chapter 1 : Night-Time Nurturers

Recipe 57 : Relaxing Vanilla Lavender Smoothie

Unwind in the evening with the "Relaxing Vanilla Lavender Smoothie," a serene blend for nighttime nourishment. This high-protein smoothie combines the soothing qualities of lavender with the comforting flavor of vanilla, creating a perfect beverage for relaxation. Ideal as a pre-sleep treat or a calming end to your day, it's a gentle way to support your body's nighttime recovery and relaxation.

- **Servings**: 1 (One)
- **Prepping Time**: 5 Minutes
- **Cook Time**: 0 Minutes
- **Difficulty**: Easy

INGREDIANT

- 1 scoop vanilla protein powder
- 1 cup almond milk
- 1/2 tsp dried lavender (edible grade)
- 1 tbsp honey or agave nectar
- A dash of vanilla extract
- Ice cubes (optional)

NUTRITIONAL FACTS: (PER SERVING)

Calories: 300	Protein: 25g
Carbohydrates: 25g	Fat: 8g
Fiber: 2g	Sugar: 15g

STEP BY PREPARATION

- Blend protein powder, almond milk, lavender, honey/agave, and vanilla extract.
- Add ice cubes for a colder texture, if desired.
- Blend until smooth and fragrant.
- Serve in a glass and embrace the relaxing aroma and taste.

The "Relaxing Vanilla Lavender Smoothie" is more than a drink; it's a soothing ritual. Whether preparing for a restful sleep or simply seeking tranquility, this smoothie provides a delightful, healthful way to relax and unwind, making it an ideal addition to your evening routine.

Chapter 1 : Night-Time Nurturers

Recipe 58 : Cinnamon Nightcap Protein Smoothie

End your day with the comforting embrace of the "Cinnamon Nightcap Protein Smoothie," a warming, high-protein drink perfect for nighttime relaxation. This smoothie combines the soothing spice of cinnamon with creamy, protein-rich ingredients, creating a delightful evening treat. It's ideal for those seeking a cozy way to wind down and nourish their body before bedtime, ensuring a peaceful and restful night.

- **Servings**: 1 (One)
- **Prepping Time**: 5 Minutes
- **Cook Time**: 0 Minutes
- **Difficulty**: Easy

INGREDIANT

- ✅ 1 scoop vanilla protein powder
- ✅ 1 cup almond milk or milk of choice
- ✅ 1/2 banana, frozen
- ✅ 1 tsp ground cinnamon
- ✅ 1 tbsp almond butter
- ✅ A dash of nutmeg
- ✅ Ice cubes (optional)

NUTRITIONAL FACTS: (PER SERVING)

Calories: 350	Protein: 25g
Carbohydrates: 30g	Fat: 15g
Fiber: 4g	Sugar: 15g

STEP BY PREPARATION

- ➤ Mix protein powder, almond milk, banana, cinnamon, almond butter, and nutmeg in a blender.
- ➤ Add ice cubes for a thicker smoothie, if preferred.
- ➤ Blend until smooth and creamy.
- ➤ Pour into a glass and enjoy your soothing nightcap.

The "Cinnamon Nightcap Protein Smoothie" is more than just a beverage; it's a nighttime ritual that combines indulgence with wellness. Perfect for those who want to enjoy a tasty and comforting drink while taking care of their nutritional needs, this smoothie offers a peaceful way to conclude your day and prepare for a restful night's sleep.

Chapter 1 : Night-Time Nurturers

Recipe 59 : Blueberry Evening Elixir Smoothie

Embrace the tranquil essence of the evening with the "Blueberry Evening Elixir Smoothie," a delightful high-protein concoction perfect for winding down. This smoothie marries the sweet, antioxidant-rich blueberries with soothing protein, ideal for nighttime nourishment. It's the perfect choice for a relaxing pre-bedtime snack, offering a gentle and healthful way to end your day and prepare for a restful night.

- **Servings:** 1 (One)
- **Prepping Time:** 5 Minutes
- **Cook Time:** 0 Minutes
- **Difficulty:** Easy

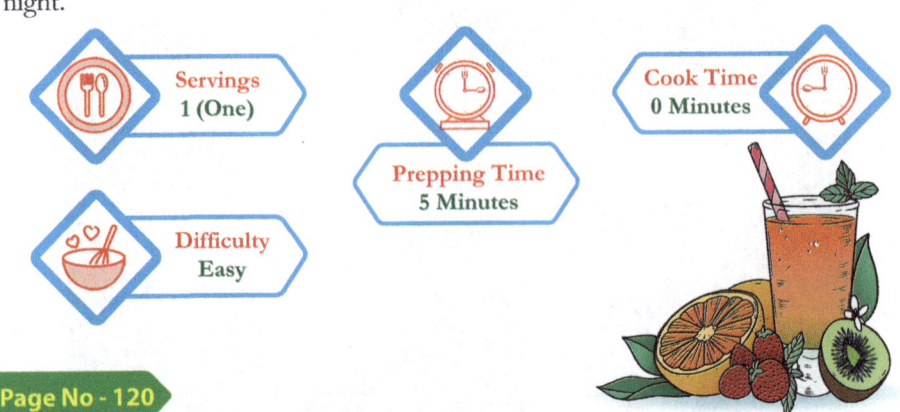

Page No - 120

INGREDIANT

- 1 scoop vanilla protein powder
- 1 cup almond milk
- 1/2 cup frozen blueberries
- 1/4 banana, frozen
- 1 tbsp Greek yogurt (or vegan alternative)
- A sprinkle of ground cinnamon
- Ice cubes (optional)

NUTRITIONAL FACTS: (PER SERVING)

Calories: 300	Protein: 25g
Carbohydrates: 30g	Fat: 5g
Fiber: 5g	Sugar: 20g

STEP BY PREPARATION

- Combine protein powder, almond milk, blueberries, banana, Greek yogurt, and cinnamon in a blender.
- Add ice cubes for a chilled texture, if preferred.
- Blend until smooth and creamy.
- Pour into a glass and relish the soothing flavors.

The "Blueberry Evening Elixir Smoothie" is more than just a drink; it's a nightly ritual of calm and care. Whether you're seeking a nutritious way to relax after a busy day or need a gentle snack before bedtime, this smoothie provides a harmonious blend of flavor and nutrition, aiding in a peaceful transition to a night of restful sleep.

Chapter 1 : Night-Time Nurturers

Recipe 60: Soothing Coconut Chocolate Smoothie

Indulge in the calming blend of the "Soothing Coconut Chocolate Smoothie," a luscious high-protein treat for nighttime serenity. This smoothie combines the comforting richness of chocolate with the tropical smoothness of coconut, creating an ideal evening delight. It's perfect for those seeking a peaceful way to end their day, offering a delicious and nutritious option to unwind before a restful night's sleep.

Servings
1 (One)

Cook Time
0 Minutes

Prepping Time
5 Minutes

Difficulty
Easy

INGREDIANT

- 1 scoop of chocolate protein powder
- 1 cup coconut milk
- 1 tbsp unsweetened cocoa powder
- 1/2 banana, frozen
- 1 tbsp shredded coconut
- A dash of vanilla extract
- Ice cubes (optional)

NUTRITIONAL FACTS: (PER SERVING)

Calories: 350	Protein: 25g
Carbohydrates: 30g	Fat: 15g
Fiber: 4g	Sugar: 15g

STEP BY PREPARATION

- Blend chocolate protein powder, coconut milk, cocoa powder, banana, shredded coconut, and vanilla extract in a blender.
- Add ice cubes for a thicker consistency, if desired.
- Blend until smooth and creamy.
- Serve in a glass garnished with a sprinkle of shredded coconut.

The "Soothing Coconut Chocolate Smoothie" is more than just a beverage; it's a delightful way to embrace the evening. Perfect for those who crave a sweet yet healthful treat at night, this smoothie offers an ideal balance of taste and nutrition, helping you to relax and prepare for a peaceful night's sleep.

Conclusion

As we conclude "Easy High Protein Smoothie Recipes Book: Quick & Healthy Blends with Original Ideas & Stunning Photos" by Lily Johnson, we hope you feel inspired and equipped to incorporate these nutritious and delicious smoothies into your daily routine. Lily's passion for healthy living shines through every recipe, each designed to offer a perfect blend of taste, nutrition, and convenience.

Whether you're a fitness enthusiast looking for post-workout recovery drinks, someone interested in weight management, or simply seeking to boost your daily protein intake, this book has provided various options to suit your needs. The stunning photos accompanying each recipe make this book a visual treat and serve as a guide to creating picture-perfect smoothies every time.

Remember, every sip is a step towards a healthier, more energetic you. We encourage you to experiment with these recipes, make them your own, and never hesitate to share the joy of healthy living with others. Thank you for choosing this journey with Lily Johnson. Here's to enjoying every blend and transforming your health, one smoothie at a time.

THANK YOU

Made in the USA
Coppell, TX
14 January 2025